REVEALING *the* INNER
WORLD *of* TRAUMATISED
CHILDREN *and* YOUNG PEOPLE

of related interest

Healing Child Trauma Through Restorative Parenting
A Model for Supporting Children and Young People
Dr Chris Robinson and Terry Philpot
ISBN 978 1 84905 699 1
eISBN 978 1 78450 215 7

Creative Therapies for Complex Trauma
Helping Children and Families in Foster Care, Kinship Care or Adoption
Edited by Anthea Hendry and Joy Hasler
Foreword by Colwyn Trevarthen
ISBN 978 1 78592 005 9
eISBN 978 1 78450 242 3

**A Therapeutic Treasure Box for Working with Children
and Adolescents with Developmental Trauma**
Creative Techniques and Activities
Dr. Karen Treisman
ISBN 978 1 78592 263 3
eISBN 978 1 78450 553 0

Counselling Skills for Working with Trauma
Healing From Child Sexual Abuse, Sexual Violence and Domestic Abuse
Christiane Sanderson
ISBN 978 1 84905 326 6
eISBN 978 0 85700 743 8

Cognitive Behavioural Therapy for Child Trauma and Abuse
A Step-by-Step Approach
Jacqueline S. Feather and Kevin R. Ronan
ISBN 978 1 84905 086 9
eISBN 978 0 85700 263 1

Trauma is Really Strange
Steve Haines
Art by Sophie Standing
ISBN 978 1 84819 293 5
eISBN 978 0 85701 240 1

REVEALING *the* INNER WORLD *of* TRAUMATISED CHILDREN *and* YOUNG PEOPLE

*An Attachment-Informed Model for Assessing
Emotional Needs and Treatment*

CHRISTINE BRADLEY
with
FRANCIA KINCHINGTON

Foreword by Judith Trowell

Jessica Kingsley *Publishers*
London and Philadelphia

First published in 2018
by Jessica Kingsley Publishers
73 Collier Street
London N1 9BE, UK
and
400 Market Street, Suite 400
Philadelphia, PA 19106, USA

www.jkp.com

Library of Congress Cataloging in Publication Data
Names: Bradley, Christine (Christine Mary), 1945- author. | Kinchington,
    Francia, author. | Trowell, Judith, writer of foreword.
Title: Revealing the inner world of traumatised children and young people :
    an attachment-informed model for assessing emotional needs and treatment /
    Christine Bradley with Francia Kinchington ; foreword by Judith Trowell.
Description: London ; Philadelphia : Jessica Kingsley Publishers, 2018. |
    Includes bibliographical references and index.
Identifiers: LCCN 2017041194 | ISBN 9781785920196 (alk. paper)
Subjects: | MESH: Neurodevelopmental Disorders--therapy | Battered Child
    Syndrome--psychology | Psychotherapy--methods | Community Mental Health
    Services | Community Integration | Child | Adolescent | England

British Library Cataloguing in Publication Data
A CIP catalogue record for this book is available from the British Library

ISBN 978 1 78592 019 6
eISBN 978 1 78450 265 2

Printed and bound in Great Britain

This book is dedicated to my mother and the children with whom I have had the privilege to work with over the years

Contents

Part 2. Applying the Concepts in Different Settings

Foreword

This book came about as a result of Christine Bradley's passion to pass on what she has learned and understood about working with emotionally traumatised children. The roots of her work lie with Barbara Dockar-Drysdale (psychotherapist, founder of the Mulberry Bush School, Oxfordshire, and therapeutic consultant to the Cotswold Community, Wiltshire), with whom she worked, and, subsequently, Donald Winnicott (paediatrician and psychoanalyst). She is a respected professional who has worked in the field of psychotherapy and social work, both nationally and internationally, and as a trainer and consultant to local authorities and children's organisations over the past 40 years.

What is impressive about the book is how the context for each child is explained. This elaborates on the circumstances in which these troubled children and young people are brought up, how they present and the dilemmas for professionals trying to help them.

The book is prefaced by the experience of the Cotswold Community, which helps set the context for the detail that follows. The Community was built on a foundation of psychoanalytic theory and the concepts of integration/unintegration to provide opportunities for young people, giving them a second chance. John Whitwell recounts how the Community depended on staff who had the capacity to bear the intense emotional pain, agony, rage and longing that emerged. Working there was life-changing for both the staff and the young people.

Part 1 commences with Alistair Cooper, who brings together theory and practice to deepen our understanding of the impact of adverse circumstances on children and young people. He gives a contemporary theoretical perspective to the book.

This leads into the following chapters where Christine Bradley shares her understanding and insight gained over a lifetime in practice working with troubled children who are struggling in society. These chapters provide an in-depth understanding of the children's difficulties and, importantly, need assessment and treatment. The more common presentations of the frozen child, the archipelago child, the caretaker child and the fragile integrated child are discussed and analysed in the accompanying tables. The core throughout is a profound understanding and use of psychoanalytic and attachment theories.

Part 2 examines current provision and ways forward. With this book, we now have ideas for how this knowledge and understanding can be used in community settings and the places in the community that care for these children, whether this is in foster care or in specialist placements. The Mulberry Bush School, discussed by John Diamond in Chapter 9, is one of the few remaining therapeutic residential settings where very troubled youngsters are given support in developing, socialising, building relationships and gaining an education.

The struggle to manage these children is intense and demanding. Some of these children go on to be adopted, and provision has developed from adoption to post-adoption services, supporting families that offer a home and a substitute family. Often these children and young people are given a label of attachment disorder; while this is all right as far as it goes, one is left thinking about how to proceed. Foster carers and social workers will find the ideas in this book helpful as they endeavour to work with these children and young people to form relationships. Underpinning all this is the need for good supervision and timely consultation – for foster carers, social workers, teachers and residential workers. This is spelt out in the book in a helpful way. Without good supervision, professionals flounder, foster carers and adoptive parents become despairing and placements break down or children are excluded.

This book provides pathways to enable the children and young people to be seen as developing and growing rather than being written off. All the children across these placements are entitled to education, whether this is in school, college, pupil referral unit or special school. Teachers, class teachers, teaching assistants and special educational needs teachers will find this book helpful as they try to understand and work with these children. It is important that nursery schools recognise these children at an early stage, and the book will help them to devise ways forward. In addition to educators, adolescent mental health settings see many of these young people for advice and sometimes treatment. This book, then, is of importance to a wide range of society, including parents, professionals and educators in higher education.

The book shows the relevance to the 21st century of the pioneering work that took place in the 1970s and 1980s, where there was time to think and discuss with colleagues to form an in-depth understanding of each child. It is a distillation of the knowledge, insight and understanding that Christine Bradley has accumulated during her lengthy career; how wonderful that it will not be lost! I hope this book will encourage a rediscovery of this way of working.

Preface: The Cotswold Community

The Story of a Pioneering Therapeutic Community

John Whitwell

I have been privileged to have worked with severely emotionally disturbed children and young people for over 40 years. I joined the staff of the Cotswold Community in 1972 at a time when the approved school era had come to an end with the 1969 Children and Young Person's Act and the appointment of Richard Balbernie as Principal in 1967. His focus and vision drew together a team of experienced and far-sighted individuals, including Barbara Dockar-Drysdale, Isabel Menzies-Lyth (a psychoanalyst and one of the pioneers who formed The Tavistock Institute in London) and Eric Miller (a social scientist with expertise in organisational theory and an early staff member of The Tavistock Institute). Their pioneering approaches contributed to the creation of a unique therapeutic environment. When I took over from Balbernie as Principal in 1985, the Cotswold Community was very well established as a therapeutic environment for the recovery of emotionally unintegrated children (who have not achieved a separate, coherent sense of self), and it had a deserved international reputation. We successfully navigated the handover from the founder leader and the founder consultant psychotherapist to Paul Van Heeswyk, and the culture continued to flourish. I left in 1999.

Historical context

The transformation of the original Cotswold Approved School into the Cotswold Community came at a time when the writing was on the wall for approved schools. An increasing number of scandals had hit the headlines, which together with their low success rate had brought the approved school regime into disrepute. This was true for the original Cotswold – the description of conditions that came out was chilling. The living conditions for the boys were harsh and cramped, they were subject to appalling initiation ceremonies and younger and smaller boys were subject to bullying and sexual assault. The three houses in the 'polytechnic' special school became known as 'Butlins, Bedlam and Belsen'. Approved schools fundamentally failed to create environments where young people could change in a way that would be useful in their rehabilitation.

The Rainer Foundation, the managing body of the Cotswold School, anticipated the changes that were on the horizon and took this opportunity to find a leader for the school with qualities that would enable a change in culture. This vision was predicated on the creation of a school that provided a therapeutic community (a planned environment based on psychodynamic principles), offering a total treatment plan involving remedial and social education; a positive group living experience; individual and family casework; and community links. Derek Morrell, the Under Secretary of State at the Home Office at the time, whose vision and philosophy lay behind the 1969 Children Act which abolished approved schools, recognised the enormity of what was required to transform the existing system into one that worked for the young people involved. He acknowledged the need to establish creative pioneering work that could be transferred into the general system.

David Wills' book *Spare the Child* (Wills 1971b) detailed the transformation of the Cotswold School into the Cotswold Community. It described how Richard Balbernie recognised the importance of specialist psychological and research-informed practice and returned to education to gain a degree in psychology and train as a teacher, educational psychologist and psychotherapist.

Balbernie himself acknowledged the value of his previous experience of trying to establish a therapeutic community at Swaylcliffe Park as vitally important in the ultimate success of his leadership at the Cotswold Community. He was under no illusion about how hard the transformation would be. In his book *Residential Work with Children*, published in 1966, a year before he became Principal of the Cotswold Community, Balbernie set out his manifesto for the residential treatment of children, stating:

Neurotic children capable of a transference require individual psychotherapy and a special and supportive educational setting; pre-neurotic children (those not having achieved ego integration and often stuck at a more primitive level of object identification) require a totally controllable and controlled environment wholly adapted to their needs and where special and skilled consultation and support for staff and special resources of consciousness are available, since, in such cases, the worker has to see the child through the equivalent of very early and primitive interaction processes and provide symbolically the psychic reality of very early missed experience while the child is in a very regressed, totally dependent, state. (Balbernie 1966: 53–54)

Key to his philosophy was the need to create an ordered environment that enabled therapy to take place, a setting that enabled pre-neurotic or unintegrated children to be themselves, to feel accepted as they were, and to feel relaxed and less pressurised rather than anxious and frightened. The aim in this special environment was to build up real strengths and personal achievements and, eventually, independence, through finding and accepting weak, lost or difficult parts of themselves. In a disordered environment, an unintegrated child would fall headlong into an increasing spiral of acting out their most primitive feelings, which neither they nor their environment could contain.

The transformation

Balbernie called on his friends of many years, Barbara Dockar-Drysdale and Michael Fitzgerald, who worked for the London Boroughs' Children's Regional Planning Committee. Dockar-Drysdale was a psychotherapist with a national and international reputation, which started with her work with 'maladjusted' children at the Mulberry Bush School, founded with her husband some 20 years previously. Their value to the new Cotswold Community was a theoretical philosophy grounded in extensive experience, a fact recognised by sceptical staff. Dockar-Drysdale (known affectionately as Mrs D, a term I will use in the rest of this preface) was held in high regard. During the time that Wills spent at the Cotswold Community, researching material for his book, he was constantly reminded of her by staff, including ancillary staff, who acknowledged the value of her insight and work.

Balbernie defined the new primary task of the Cotswold Community. It is very clear that this was strongly influenced by the consultant input of A.K. Rice, who wrote *Working Note No. 1* (1968), the first in a series of working notes arising from the Tavistock Institute consultancy. Rice wrote:

> More understanding of delinquency has led to the view that delinquency itself is a presenting symptom of psychological damage and disturbance. The important questions that have to be answered if therapy is to be successful are: What is damaged? How is the disturbance caused? and, What is successful therapy? (Rice 1968:6)

Dockar-Drysdale (1973), in her paper 'Staff Consultation in an Evolving Care System', described the struggle to establish a therapeutic culture at the Cotswold Community. She battled with three key obstacles:

- *'The theory of the impossible task'* that any change that occurred could only be superficial. This idea was subscribed to by families, institutions and management where child care workers were attributed a heroic role, as people making great sacrifices in order to devote themselves to a hopeless but worthy cause, and the children themselves were seen as 'helpless and hopeless', a dynamic that Mrs D was also drawn into.

- *'The Dinosaurs'*, which she defined as a subculture of institutionalisation based on past hierarchical structures. There were many adults and boys who believed that the change was momentary and that the old order would be restored before long. The Dinosaurs embodied the legacy of all the parts of the institution that stayed with people whose identity was defined by their past roles and where the institution had played a central role in their lives.

- *'The fallacy of a delusional equilibrium'*. This was another basic assumption on the part of many people in the institution, which implied that, by keeping things calm and smooth on top, the chaos below the surface need not be reached. Breakdown in this false equilibrium was projected on to any likely scapegoat who was often then ejected, whether it was a boy or an adult.

Balbernie and Mrs D initially assumed that the majority of the boys at the Cotswold Community would be emotionally integrated, albeit in a fragile way. They found that when they first classified all the boys in the Community, on the basis of integration as individuals,

75 per cent of the population turned out to be unintegrated. A house was then set up for the integrated 25 per cent. This unit would accept boys who had achieved integration as a result of treatment within the Community as well as the very few who, on referral, seemed to be integrated.

Dockar-Drysdale gave a vivid description of the nature of her consultancy with the staff teams and individual staff members. Establishing a therapeutic culture was no easy matter, and the changes were incremental rather than dramatic.

> Initially, subject matter for team discussion groups depended entirely on what they themselves surfaced. I felt that they were under such stress that my chief value at first must be as a safety valve in what was a crisis culture. There was mass acting-out in all units, and subculture among staff as well as boys. Workers, both in groups and individually, selected communication to impart to me in a way which made it very difficult to be of any use. The fallacy of the delusional equilibrium was much in evidence: information concerning the various units gave the impression of a smooth-running, well established organisation, only disturbed by the not-to-be-explained phenomena of acting out, which could not be denied. (1973:43)

Mrs D observed that the process of classifying boys as 'integrated' or 'unintegrated' did much to open up dialogue. In order to answer the key questions for this approach, 'Does this boy panic?' and 'Does he disrupt?', workers started to ask themselves new questions both about boys and about themselves. To make use of this development Mrs D evolved a technique which she called 'need assessment'. This focused the attention of the whole group, including the consultant, on the primary task, namely the provision of primary experience.

Mrs D believed that anti-task, acting out and subcultures of all kinds sprung from a breakdown in real communication. Therefore, it was of the utmost importance to keep all lines of communication open: between members of the team; between adults and children; and between the consultant and others in the organisation. Creating a need assessment involves the whole staff group of a residential house working with the consultant to pool resources to evaluate need. Insights were often reached in the making of these assessments that were not only of value to the child under consideration, but also to the treatment team themselves, throwing light on problems such as splitting mechanisms (where a child consciously or unconsciously creates a divide within the staff team), which were managed in a way that was tolerable because it was indirect and shared. Such an approach recognised the value of child care workers as an integral part of the professional team.

Mrs D observed that, as the unit teams became accustomed to using need assessments, there was a considerable opening up of communication. For the first time, people began to take some share of responsibility for acting out by the boys. Mrs D felt it was safe to say repeatedly that all acting out resulted from a breakdown in communication. However, the exception to this could be found in symbolic acting out in relation to an adult. The distinction she made was that 'symbolic acting out' took the form of a message or communication whereby the individual expressed their feelings either in a physical or non-verbal way. Importantly, this was always directed to a known and trusted person. In contrast 'acting out' was defined as a breakdown in communication that did not take place in the context of a relationship.

Mrs D stressed the need for staff to be resilient and open to the continuous development of self-awareness, pointing out that people working with unintegrated children and adolescents had to carry a much heavier load of tension and anxiety than those who were trying to help neurotic, integrated youngsters.

> Workers at the Cotswold are constantly exposed to the full blast of primary processes – they are in touch with what should be in the unconscious but which, without ego development, is present at a conscious level in all its primitive violence (Winnicott used to describe this as 'dreaming awake'). The danger – apart from the actual violent acting out – is that this primitive material can pick up wavelengths in the unconscious of the workers – this is what can lead to collusive pairing, which is damaging in the extreme to boy and adult. For these reasons it is essential that workers should become as conscious as possible about themselves, so that they and the boys are less at risk and more free to concentrate on the primary task. (Dockar-Drysdale 1973:47)

Mrs D described how there could be a collision between objective and inner reality and illustrated it as follows:

Jim, a boy at the Cotswold, became interested in chess, so that presently he wished to carve a chess set. He made a king, a queen and a pawn, which he brought to show me. His instructor told me that he now refused to complete the set. However, Jim had – from his point of view – completed another kind of set: a father, a mother and a child – the family life he had never known. It is difficult for workers to accept this other kind of reality, especially when there is such a clash of interests and investment. (Dockar-Drysdale 1973:52)

But lest you might be thinking this really is an impossible task, Mrs D spelled out the positives and achievements that she facilitated. She stressed that the workers in the Cotswold Community reached a very high standard of therapeutic work, which many people supposed could only be carried out by psychotherapists. But nothing, she felt, could be further from the case, for despite the pains of gaining insight and the acute anxiety aroused by accepting responsibility in the deepest sense for other people's acting out, the staff in the Community continued to tolerate a learning process that demanded so much of them. They continued to work in a way that called for respect and admiration. The changes and evolvement in the boys, which took place as a result of their efforts, could be seen clearly in later need assessments, giving the workers a satisfaction greater than anything they had experienced in the past.

Therapeutic management

When the regime of the Cotswold Approved School came to an end and Richard Balbernie started the transformation towards a therapeutic community, chaos ensued. The old order offered stability, in that suppression seemed better than anarchy. So it was at the Cotswold Community in the early days.

What changed? It took time for a new kind of order to become established, one not based on fear of punishment or being bullied but on the development of the personal authority of the workers. This didn't happen magically but through the workers being tested and discovering that they could survive the young people's disturbance. I think the following story shared with me by a female Cotswold Community worker illustrates this process.

I walked into his bedroom to do his bedtime visit and Trevor was frantically putting on several layers of clothing, including five pairs of socks. I told him that I would not just let him run off in such a state. He went to the window. I explained it was cold, dark and wet outside and that I would take hold of his hand if he started to climb out of the window. Knowing this boy very well, I predicted openly what may follow. I said that if he went to scratch me I would have to take hold of him so that he couldn't scratch. I went further to explain that if he then went to kick I would then have to take hold of him fully. I re-stated that I really did not want him to run off.

The holding felt inevitable, but at each stage I was able to clearly state what would happen next and explain that I would be with him until it was over.

There came a point during the holding when he became so desperate to go outside for some fresh air. I felt I had to respect this. Before I let go I explained that as before I did not want him running off and would stay with him. He went through the French doors and walked a short distance with me closely behind. He then looked up in astonishment saying, 'My feet are wet!' I explained that socks are not waterproof, so it did not matter how many layers you had on. He said his feet were cold, so I asked if he wanted me to pick him up, [and] he nodded. I held him across my hip, as you would a toddler.

It is worth noting that when I let go he called me by his natural mother's name and did not want me even holding his hand. At this next stage we carried on in the same direction, as if we were mother and infant. I turned round and he anxiously said that he did not want to go back inside. I replied, 'You don't feel ready', but explained we would have to go back in as it was getting late, but not yet.

Trevor looked up at the moon and started asking questions about the universe, God, spirits and witches. We discussed all these things with me carrying him back and forth, the length of the house. We were getting very wet but neither of us noticed. He then spoke about being held. He said he felt safe when he was held, but not when I held him, as I was his [focal] carer. He explained that he did not feel safe because he scratched and bit me. I said he did not want to hurt me. He stroked the scratches on my hand as he said this. I went over why I had held and how it had come about.

We chatted some more about this and that and I suggested it was time to go back in, he agreed and got changed for bed. I tucked him in with a hot water bottle. He held my hand affectionately and we said goodnight. (Whitwell 1998:93–94)

It's worth bearing in mind that this episode took place in a group living context and that there were other workers with the rest of the group who were getting on with their bedtime routine without being drawn into Trevor's disturbance. In the early days of the Community, this episode would very likely have led to a group merger with other boys being drawn towards Trevor's disturbance like moths to light. In the approved school era, this episode would never have been allowed to run its course. It would have been seen primarily as a disciplinary matter and 'dealt with' accordingly.

The Community did not have a system of punishments and rewards to control children because having children 'under control' was not our primary task. As therapists, we were more interested in the meaning of behaviour rather than simply controlling it. If a child behaved in an anti-social way we wanted to know why and, ultimately, we wanted the child to understand why, because a gain in insight by the child would lead to a change in behaviour. For instance, if one understands why one is driven to steal, it is no longer possible to steal with impunity. We were not interested in children behaving well while residing in the Community and then falling apart once they'd left.

An emotionally unintegrated child has very few inner controls. His behaviour is impulsive as emotionally he is a baby or toddler and in need of almost constant support and supervision. When children first came to the Community this was the nature of our work – we called it therapeutic management. It brought together the emotionally disturbed child's need for therapy and management. It was not possible for one to succeed without the other. A 'carrot and stick' approach was not only irrelevant but would not have worked as the unintegrated child did not have sufficient ego strength to be able to learn from experience, hence the repeated senseless anti-social behaviour.

The task of the residential therapist is to make a judgement about what the child can manage at any moment in time. Giving him more space than he can manage is inviting breakdown. However, where the child feels emotionally stronger but is not given the opportunity to use this, a growth opportunity is missed and the child feels frustrated. Knowing a child sufficiently well to make this judgement takes a good deal of skill on the part of the residential therapist and is one of the creative aspects of the role, as no manual can provide all the answers. Over a period, our aim was for the child to become emotionally stronger so that he could take over some of this responsibility for himself, i.e. to move from a position of having few inner controls and needing to be managed, to a position where he had increasing self-control and needed minimal management.

Our view was that a disturbed, chaotic child needs to be in an ordered, integrated environment to hold all the fragmented aspects of himself together. In the Cotswold Community, it was possible for a child to be looked after, to play and to go to school, all in the one environment. If there was a problem in one part of his life, everyone knew straight away; for example, if he had a difficult afternoon in the school, the adults who worked with him in the evening would know about this and could continue to work with him on the problem. This is often not the case in our society where it is quite likely for a child to have a problem at school for weeks before it is communicated to his parents and vice versa. This situation is not sufficiently containing for unintegrated children who will inevitably exploit the gap by creating 'splits' between the different groups of adults in their lives. A boy at the Cotswold Community would not have got away with working these splits for long.

If a person has not developed the capacity to distinguish between what is 'inside' and 'outside' himself and isn't able to control the boundary between them, then he needs to be in an environment where there are clearly defined and simple boundaries. Working with emotionally disturbed people requires clear definitions with regard to individuals, groups and systems and their boundaries. In many respects the therapy is the 'order' of the organisation and, importantly, the ego-functioning and behaviour of the staff. The milieu, the whole management structure, needs to reinforce and support this; if contradicted, it will re-enact and echo the children's earliest environmental failures and breakdowns.

Food and therapy

Perhaps the biggest contrast between the approved school era and what followed at the Cotswold Community can be seen in how food was viewed and managed. The approved school had a central kitchen and dining room where all the meals were eaten. The task was to feed the boys 'en masse' as efficiently as possible with the minimum of 'incidents'. Managing a dining room of 120 adolescent boys was no easy task for the staff, and staff were ranked according to their ability to deal with this situation. The skills needed in small-group living are very different.

Mrs D introduced to the staff of the Community the therapeutic importance of food and feeding. This is at the heart of therapeutic relationships, as it is between small children and their parents. Isabel Menzies-Lyth advised the Community to close the central kitchen and develop a kitchen in each of the households so that mealtimes could more closely resemble a family situation. Boys became involved in the preparation of meals, and the wastage of food dropped considerably as meals became more appetising. Importantly, feelings about food and what it represented, which is often central in therapeutic work, could now be worked on more meaningfully in the home.

The symbolic importance of food became a part of the therapeutic culture. As unintegrated boys started to become attached to their focal carer, small adaptations were being made. Mrs D related this to the adaptations that parents naturally make to their babies and toddlers. However, with 12-year-olds this might take the form of a special drink at bedtime or a particular biscuit or fruit when he returns from school.

Mrs D also postulated that delinquent excitement could be converted into oral greed. A good example of this concerned Gavin, who came to the Community when he was 13 years old. He was an established delinquent having been to court on numerous occasions charged with theft. He was also addicted to smoking and, unknown to us initially, hid plastic bags of tobacco and cigarettes in the grounds. He regularly left the household in the middle of the night to retrieve a bag. When he ran out he walked to the nearest pub (three miles away) to rummage in their bins for cigarette ends. Despite numerous exhortations to wake the grown-up sleeping in the household, he continued with this practice and it was clear that the excitement he felt when involved in this clandestine activity was as addictive as the tobacco.

The staff team spent much time discussing him with Mrs D. Gradually more was discovered about his very early childhood. He had been hospitalised several times because of a 'failure to thrive' and had instantly put on weight when reliably cared for. Mrs D helped the team to appreciate what it would have felt like for such a young child to be severely neglected. Probably he would have woken in the night feeling very hungry but receiving no response to his cries. Eventually he would give up and expect to be ignored. The staff team, having taken this on board, developed the hypothesis that his current night-time activity was an attempt at self-provision. No wonder, since he had no confidence in getting a response from the staff member sleeping in the household.

With the guidance of Mrs D, his focal carer started to explore this with Gavin and suggested to him that he could be woken during the night and be given a 'feed'. Gavin was astounded that anyone would do this for him, and initially he went along with this suggestion out of curiosity and scepticism. For several weeks, Gavin was woken in the night with something to eat, something he had chosen. The fear for workers making this kind of adaptation is that it will last forever. It doesn't, because when the need has been met the adaptation becomes redundant and the child moves on. Gavin was able to say when he no longer felt the need for it. In the early days of the adaptation he tested out the commitment of the staff by having the night feed and then clandestinely going out of the household as before (having his cake and eating it!). Gradually this dropped away, as at an emotional level, he was getting what he needed.

Nowadays there is much focus on the nutritional aspect of food for children, which is undoubtedly important, but the emotional significance of food is often neglected or not even realised. We all now know what is meant by 'comfort food', but this was an important insight in the development of the therapeutic culture at the Cotswold Community. Dockar-Drysdale summarised this point well in her paper 'The Difference between Child Care and Therapeutic Management':

> The differences between child care and therapeutic involvement are best seen by comparing the two kinds of work within the framework of everyday life. For example, child care workers know a lot about food and just what children need to keep them well[;] therapeutic workers…, while they are aiming to provide a balanced diet, are tuned into the emotional needs of the child where food is under consideration. (1988:8)

Play and communication

Communication was fundamental to the therapeutic work at the Cotswold Community. Emotionally disturbed children need to be helped to communicate how they feel, since failure to do this leads to the acting out of those feelings through anti-social and violent behaviour. It is important that children are offered non-verbal models of communication, as their ability to put feelings into words is often inhibited and some of the unconscious feelings may belong to a pre-verbal era of their lives.

The profound benefits of play can be seen most clearly in the lives of those whose capacity to play has been suppressed or distorted as a result of trauma or deprivation. In such cases, play itself can be an extremely effective method of healing, for play, like dreams, serves the function of self-revelation and of communication at a deep level. This is the central premise behind play therapy. Using play as both the vehicle and the cure for psychological distress, play therapists aim to break the destructive circularity of that distress. At the Cotswold Community, play was highly valued. One of the central tenets was that play is a vital ingredient in well-being. Playing was an essential part of the emotional work that the boys had to do, and this was reflected in the daily timetable, which gave as much time to play as to school work.

However, many of the boys were unable to play, or rather the play they engaged in was as disturbed as they were. Mock-fighting often escalated into real fighting; competitive games could quickly become unbearably stressful; even relatively gentle fantasy play with toys could feel quite threatening to these children whose own lives had provided so little of the safety and stability that are the necessary pre-conditions for play.

In the Community's supportive environment, the boys were given the opportunity to discover a way of playing that was not destructive to either themselves or others. This process of self-discovery through play was extremely powerful. The boys were able to regress to the age at which they 'lost themselves' and, as it were, start again. A 13-year-old may retreat to the age of a three- or four-year-old in which he clings to his teddy bear and uses it to communicate to the world. There is nothing unusual in asking a toddler what Teddy would like for tea, but addressing a 13-year-old in this way is a poignant reminder of the necessity of childhood play – as necessary to our future well-being as learning to walk or talk. The example of Peter below illustrates the importance of symbolic communication for children who have been emotionally damaged at a pre-verbal stage of development, and consequently struggle to put their feelings into words.

Peter came to the Community when he was ten. He seldom spoke and seemed locked away inside his head, from where he viewed the world with unconcealed distrust and fear. The only clue he gave to his inner state were the pictures that he was constantly drawing. There were several striking features about these pictures: they were always of a town encircled by high, thick walls, drawn in heavy grey or black crayon; inside the town there were a few buildings dotted about but there were no streets or paths to connect them. On the outside of the wall a few wiggly roads led to the perimeter of the town but no further, for there were never any gates in Peter's drawings either into or out of the town.

For a long time, Peter's pictures, or 'maps' as he called them, remained unchanged. But very gradually they began to acquire new features. More streets and pathways appeared inside the town, connecting up the different buildings; more roads appeared outside the town too, so that there were now several approach routes; a small gateway appeared on the south side of the town, although no roads as yet led directly to or from it.

The residential therapist working with Peter let him discuss the design and detail of his maps without making an attempt to connect them to his psychological state. The turning point came one evening when the therapist came across a bundle of papers tied up in a plastic bag and dumped in the outside dustbin. The bundle turned out to be Peter's latest maps, hurriedly rejected for what they might reveal. And indeed, they were revealing. He had drawn a town that resembled the maps of medieval London, bustling and teeming with life and laced with a thick network of roads. And, most startling of all, at the four compass points, there were now four gateways, permitting access to and from the town. Peter himself recognised this as a turning point, hence his frightened reaction to this new world he'd discovered. Nevertheless, it signalled the start of his recovery from his psychic wounds and his gradual return to the world.

Further evidence that play is a fundamental part of therapeutic care would have been found in the Peper Harow therapeutic community which flourished alongside the Cotswold Community in the 1970s and 1980s. It had also been an approved school and was transformed into a therapeutic community under the leadership of Melvyn Rose in 1978 (Rose 1990). During the first year, new members of the community, did not attend mainstream school. Instead, learning took place within the community with the emphasis placed on play and creativity. This enforced leisure was challenging for the young people but eventually led to enhanced self-motivation so that when they did eventually return to the academic world their learning took off and the results were remarkable.

The organisation as therapist

From the very beginning of the Cotswold Community, Balbernie was aware of the need for the whole organisation to support the new therapeutic primary task. However, initially the Community was like an archipelago, with islands of therapeutic work in a sea of subculture, taking several years to join up to form a genuinely therapeutic culture. Once this had been achieved, we felt it was important to keep the dynamics of the organisation under constant review. What were the boys projecting onto staff and vice versa? How far was the violence displayed by one individual a product of the group? The staff needed to be aware of the dynamics between the households and between the households and the school. A culture of continuous self-examination was necessary, and this was supported by external consultants.

The farm that we established played an important role in the therapeutic culture. It was an example of productive work or an island of sanity when the rest of the community was bogged down in raw emotions. Boys benefited from helping with farm activities, including looking after animals. Awareness of the cycle of seasons and of animals' life cycles was symbolically very valuable for their personal development. Through the existence of the farm, the territory of the Community was greatly enlarged (350 acres), providing a safe space. We may have sensed it then, but didn't have the evidence that neuroscience now provides about the therapeutic benefits potentially provided by a 'green' environment. Surely the time spent by the boys outside on the land and alongside animals contributed significantly to their healing.

Staff and their families lived on the campus. For the boys, it was reassuring that staff were not far away, and also beneficial to observe, and sometimes be in contact with, staff in their family roles. The Cotswold Community was a therapeutic village, which in time became the setting for a therapeutic organisation.

The legacy

From approximately the year 2000, for a range of reasons, the therapeutic culture and practice of the Cotswold Community altered. Referrals reduced and the Community was not financially viable. The organisation running the enterprise at this time, Action for Children, decided, in the interests of economy in 2011, to sell the site and allocate the remaining boys to another of their schools, together with any staff who wished to transfer.

Thankfully, the work lives on through the generations of staff who were inspired by being involved in such creative therapeutic care and education. They have taken the insights gained while at the Cotswold Community on to many different areas of work with young people. Some became child psychotherapists, psychologists, counsellors, managers of children's services, managers of children's homes, social workers and teachers. Many said that working at the Community gave their work grounding and provided a powerful influence throughout their careers. There was a gathering to mark the end of the Cotswold Community, to which several middle-aged men, who had been boys there, spoke about how the quality of the care they received while there had had a profound influence on the way they now looked after their own children. If the cycle of deprivation had been broken for any of the boys who came to the Community, this would indeed be a lasting legacy to treasure.

Acknowledgments

My thanks to the people who have supported and influenced me during the writing of this book and to whom I will always be grateful for their long-standing patience!

To Patrick Tomlinson for his contribution, advice and guidance in developing the book and his input on neuroscience. His experience and knowledge have been much valued.

To Francia Kinchington for her guidance, insight and expertise.

To Laura Steckley from the University of Strathclyde for her support and guidance during the early part of the book.

To June O'Neil for giving me her support and enthusiasm about the book as I was getting it started, for which I am eternally grateful.

To Judith Trowell and Jonathan Stanley for their continued support, expertise and willingness to read and re-read chapters.

To Annie Bousfield, John Clegg, Sue Norrington and Geoff Gildersleeve for reading many of the chapters and offering sound advice about their content and changes needed. Heather Geddes for her thoughts and advice about therapeutic education.

To the following people and organisations for allowing me to use clinical examples of children with whom I have worked with over the years:

- Mark Thomas and his team at ISP Child Care

- Yvonne Miller, Services Manager, and her team at Monteagle Holibrook House, London

- Dawn Ives and Alex Hyland and the team at My Choice Children's Homes, Sussex

- Simon Bayliss, Director of Little Acorns and his residential team, Kent

- Ross Barnett, Director of Channels and Choices with his team, Kent

- Nick Barnett, Director of Caldecott Foundation Kent and his team.

With thanks for the support and encouragement from the long-suffering Stephen Jones and his editorial team, Alexandra and Jane at JKP.

Finally but most importantly, to my daughter Katrina, son-in-law Jamie and grandchildren, Milly and Maisie, who in spite of my long absences and lack of availability continue to look forward to being with me and playing.

INTRODUCTION

Christine Bradley

This book is based on my lifetime's work in supporting emotionally fragmented children and young people as a residential worker, consultant, trainer and psychotherapist. Writing the book has reminded me about the children I have worked with over the years, some of whom are cited as case studies in the book. During the 1970s and 1980s when I was learning from my experiences in residential settings, there was room for creative solutions to address the complex behaviour of deeply traumatised children. The range of therapeutic communities which evolved during that period addressed their emotional, physical and educational needs. These provided the workers with appropriate support and supervision, enabling them to withstand some of the most difficult examples of acting out from the children and young people for whom they were responsible.

One of the main tasks during the era of therapeutic community provision was to move away from labelling children and young people and towards helping them to strengthen their own sense of self during their placement. This was exemplified in the work of the Cotswold Community, which moved from being an approved school for young offenders to a therapeutic community for adolescents, focusing on identifying and assessing their individual needs and working in a psychotherapeutic way to address them. The main task of their work was based on developing the adolescent's understanding of reality that would enable them to function in the outside world and to form attachment relationships that held a sense of trust and meaning with others. The impact of the work at the Cotswold Community was that recidivism in adolescents returning to being young offenders or in mental health situations dropped by 80 per cent (falling from

85 per cent to 5 per cent) (Miller 1986) following four years of therapeutic treatment. Although working intensively with young people in a therapeutic community may appear to be costly, it is important to acknowledge that the saving is cost-effective since the alternative may be that a young person spends significant periods of time over a number of years within the criminal justice system or in mental health settings, both of which impact on the young person and society.

Today's society is outcomes-led, driven by economic factors, and there is a lack of consensus in thinking about therapeutic work with emotionally fragmented children and young people. The focus is predominantly on short-term goals by professionals who support children and young people, with decisions being made about their future based on expediency rather than need.

Such pressure can cause a great deal of uncertainty, pressure and anxiety in workers and carers, leaving little opportunity for the creative thinking that is needed to provide a way forward for these young people. A clinical diagnosis is easier and quicker than addressing their emotional needs, but does not necessarily help them to live with or feel better about themselves. A 'quick fix' will focus on the outcome but does little for their long-term emotional development which has atrophied under the impact of their early trauma, leaving them with powerful feelings of emotional abandonment that are unbearable and unthinkable.

Without carers and professionals having the insight and understanding required to deal with the complexity and the emotional intensity which are the inevitable outcomes of working so closely with these traumatised children, both the carers themselves and children are placed at emotional risk. The workers and carers find the experience of the children and young people's behaviours difficult and at times unbearable. The inability to manage the situation can result in workers giving up and leaving, or ending the child's placement. A breakdown in the young person's placement where emotional responses and repetitive behaviours escalate can result in their return to young offenders institutions, secure units and mental health settings.

In 2005, I suffered a serious illness and accident, which was followed by a long period of extended recovery. Although difficult and painful, it did give me the opportunity to reflect on many aspects of my life, but specifically on my work and practice with emotionally fragmented children. This led me to a greater realisation about the impact on my work from my early mentors, and what I had learned from them about the importance of understanding and reaching the inner world of traumatised children. During my recovery period, a new Children's Act and new legislation entitled *Every Child Matters* was brought out. Reading it and reflecting on my early work at the Cotswold Community made me realise that although legislation is crucial in maintaining the momentum of the work, we must be careful not to use political statements to mask the knowledge and insight that inform the quality of care and treatment needed in work with emotionally traumatised children and young poeple.

I have continued to use, mainly with success, what I developed from my early years of practice and learning about meeting the emotional needs of adolescents in other settings; therefore it occurred to me that now was the time to start to bring the thinking back. We can compare a good professional experience to a good childhood one, if we internalise the memory as one that keeps us feeling better about what we have gained from the experience. It becomes a place we can develop ourselves from. We do not need to retreat back in our lives searching for something we never had. We can take it forward with us, and emotionally develop from there. This was described by Winnicott as the use of a 'transitional object' (1971:6). It can be either a teddy bear or piece of cloth representing the good enough childhood experience for a small child or a concept or idea for an older person gained from a learning process which inspired them. While the era of therapeutic community work has declined in many societies, it is the thinking, theoretical understanding and therapeutic practice that need to remain alive today. These are the experiences and ideas that have inspired this book.

The aim of the book

The aim of the book is to introduce readers to theories of therapeutic work and practice with children and young people that have been tried and tested successfully over a number of years. The concept of the unintegrated child as a precursor to attachment theory will help carers and workers to understand why some children are not yet prepared to attach themselves to another person. The impact of trauma, abuse and neglect in the early years can re-emerge through the difficult-to-manage behaviour of a child or young person throughout their life. The content of the book aims to provide carers and professionals with the knowledge and practice skills required to help them reach out to the intensity of panic, rage and unthinkable anxiety which has engulfed the inner world of children and young people, preventing them from functioning.

This book will be of interest to foster carers, social workers, residential workers, teachers, educators in higher education, psychologists, psychotherapists, child and adolescent mental health professionals, the criminal justice system and the Prison Reform Trust. It is our own insight and understanding that help us to respond in a more effective way to the children and adolescents for whom we are responsible. The contributions by John Whitwell and John Diamond describe the work, reflexivity and thoughtfulness needed if we are to continue the primary task of therapeutic work with children and adolescents, balancing the internal and external realities when developing a therapeutic community and school. They also describe what has to be endured to create change. The cultural expectations of residential care have changed in many ways, becoming harsher, and we are in danger of losing the opportunity for creative thinking about work with the young people. Regardless of the bureaucratic change that occurs, it is crucial to hold on to the understanding of working with emotionally fragmented children and adolescents so that both parties can make sense of the care and treatment presented to them. The primary task of therapeutic treatment and care needs to draw on the theoretical concept of integration and unintegration.

The heart of the book is about the care and treatment of integrated and unintegrated children and adolescents. The chapters on need assessment and therapeutic treatment programmes provide tools that workers can use to develop their practice. The case studies and examples describe how these have been used by workers to help children and young people towards successful outcomes and changes in their patterns of behaviour. Part 2 of the book discusses how theory and practice can respond flexibly, moving beyond residential care and fostering to develop work with refugee children and adolescents in multi-cultural societies. A glossary of terms is given at the end of the book to explain key terms used throughout the chapters.

Finally, the importance of this book is that it addresses the historical context of the concept of integration and unintegration and how it has been used over the years in therapeutic practice to produce good outcomes. Revisiting the concepts and practice offers professionals the opportunity to deepen their understanding of therapeutic practice and reflect on its applicability and contribution to their current practice in the 21st century.

PART I

EXPLORING INTEGRATION, UNINTEGRATION AND ATTACHMENT

A Jigsaw Puzzle in the Making

CHAPTER 1

THE DEVELOPMENT OF THE SELF THROUGH A SECURE ATTACHMENT

Alistair Cooper

Introduction

Today's society is increasingly complex, and one where social media offers access to larger communities of people but where there is less reliance on wider family networks. Immediate family networks tend to have fewer members in them, as parents increasingly raise children with little or no support from extended family. In this context, perhaps more than ever, having an ability to negotiate and flourish in our social world relies on mastering the skills of self-care, including having control over our own emotional world and the skills of understanding ourselves and others. Mentalising is the term given to this emotional understanding and attunement to the mental states of the self and others – the ability to empathise and to see things from the perspective of others, which is critical in enabling social relationships. Our ability to do this is first shaped by how we were cared for in our early primary relationships, particularly how harmonious and regulating these relationships were.

The familial context can be characterised as repeated in-situ social and emotional training exercises, wherein infants and children learn about relationships and practice and improve the different skills needed to relate to others both within and outside the family. In developmentally supportive environments, children have the advantage of relationships with trusted parents who directly help to strengthen the capacities that enable relatedness and connection. Research (Rutter 2006; Felitti and Anda 2009; Leadsom *et al.* 2013) repeatedly evidences the impact of the familial environment on developmental outcomes for children. The findings highlight the significance of early social environments and, specifically, the adults within them in creating conditions that optimise a child's development. Parents who foster curiosity and exploration of the inner worlds of both self and others build resilience in a child's inner world, which then enables the child to thrive in the outer world. So, relating to the world outside the self requires a parental focus on the inner world of the child.

When an infant lives with a family that promotes a felt sense of safety and emotional support, they immediately learn about their sense of self: what is them and what is not them. This begins a journey of understanding their psychological self, the emergence of which relies on much more than an infant's innate ability to organise their own experience (Fonagy *et al.* 2005). We are social creatures, who find ourselves in relationships with others; this makes the origin of the self by its very nature social. To form a self, it is necessary to have interactions with interested and connected caregivers, who provide certain types of experiences that will evoke the emergence of the self. For a child to develop a coherent sense of their inner world they need parents with whom they can truly connect emotionally, reflecting back their inner states so that their inner world becomes integrated and understood. I will refer to the primary caregiver as the mother on occasion within this chapter, though this should not be interpreted as an indication that primary care cannot be provided by others, for example fathers, extended family members, foster carers or nannies. I will explore the social origin of the self and how we create coherence about self and others in the social environment of the family. The outcomes can be very different depending on the nature of these interactions and how attuned a parent is to the needs of their child. I draw on my work with adolescents with whom I have had the good fortune to meet and support and who, for the purposes of this chapter, are anonymised.

The patterns of rhythm and harmony in secure relationships

What must it be like to be a newborn baby, a little person who knows nothing about the world, who cannot yet experience themselves as a separate entity and must know little about their emotional world?

Rather than being a helpless passive individual ready to be shaped by the environment, the infant brings skills, abilities and motivations to achieve the most important task, namely that of making relationships with their parents and caregivers.

Research studies on mother–infant interactions suggest that newborn babies demonstrate an inherent motivation to interact with adults (Nagy *et al.* 2013). They make gestures, lip movements, facial expressions and sounds that express what is going on inside their bodies and that relate to their interest in events in the world (Trevarthen, Delafield-Butt and Schögler 2011). An infant is interested in and takes part as a capable, active participant within enjoyable harmonious interactions with other people who take an interest, make an effort and feel pleasure joining in this dialogue and responding to their gestures (Trevarthen *et al.* 2011). Such harmonious interactions are called attuned interactions.

Researchers demonstrate that, during attuned interactions, parents and infants are not just matched emotionally and behaviourally, but also physiologically (Tronick 2007). These interactions are characterised by emotional communication where an infant leads and the mother follows; both match and synchronise inner states, and simultaneously both mother and infant adjust their attention, stimulation and arousal to each other's responses.

> Frankie, a 14-month-old infant, is interacting with his mother, and both are co-ordinating their responses. For example, they are following each other's gaze, smiling in response to each other and becoming animated in response to each other's animation. As Frankie becomes more excited, his mother smiles excitedly, responding in turn. She becomes psychobiologically attuned not so much to Frankie's overt behaviour but to the reflections of the rhythms of his internal state.

In exchanges of affective synchrony, a parent and infant each recreates an inner state similar to each other. They share what the other is feeling emotionally and physically on some level. The 'musicality' within attuned interactions, matched by both rhythm and style, happens subtly and provides an infant with an experience of being seen and heard, a felt experience that the parent is truly connecting with the child.

An attuned parent will match activity to the infant, and a' to recover quietly in periods of disengagement, so, for exam., excited feelings calm down and arousal is down-regulated and the infant becomes calmer, the parent is able to interpret this change in behaviour as non-threatening, a normal developmental need and not a sign of rejection. An attuned parent will also be more attentive to the infant's cue to re-engage and be willing to reconnect with interest and joy when the infant is ready.

Harmony and brain development

An infant's ability to actively join with the parent and take part in such meetings of emotionally matched experiences within social play suggests an innate capacity to orientate towards these events, but to what purpose? What happens within these interactions – why might they be important? Our ever-increasing understanding of neurological processes points to the experience-dependent maturation (reaching maturity) of the brain systems involved in attachment, which suggest that a baby's developing brain is designed to be moulded by the social and emotional environment it encounters. Everything about us, our brains, our minds and our bodies, is geared towards collaborating with each other. These interactions help neural connections and give substance and meaning to our entire lives. What happens within our primary attachment relationships are the crucial drivers in this neural development (Watt 2000).

The importance of this can be seen clearly when we consider that the early maturing right part of the brain, responsible for processing emotions, prevails in human infants (Schore 1994) and is shaped by the mother. She is actively engaged in emotionally laden interactions, which puts great responsibility on a mother's care at reflexive, implicit, non-verbal levels and the support she gives to the self-regulatory systems of her child. An attuned mother will intuitively and automatically react more frequently to her baby's displays of emotional expressions compared with more random movements, meaning there is a frequent matching of a mother's response to her baby's emotional experiences. A mother's intimate care provides vital regulatory functions for her child, who possesses immature, incomplete psychological organisation, and she will promote the development of brain functions that support the capacity to calm distress (Schore 1994). This is particularly important during the first three years of the child's life, or 1001 days, which are widely seen as the critical period for brain development and when there is greatest vulnerability in terms of the stress response. This relates to one of the earliest developmental tasks facing infants: to begin to manage their own stress. The effects of early stress have a particularly disabling effect on the developing child.

Babies are born with little capacity to soothe themselves and are completely dependent on adults to respond to, manage and regulate their emotions and stress. Healthy adults respond to distressed babies by trying to comfort them, and they use techniques such as holding, stroking, rocking, singing or walking up and down to calm them. Associating intense arousal with comfort and security from a consistent, contingent and reliable caregiver is fundamental to emotional regulation. The regular, sensitive provision of such comfort, combined with a timely response to physical needs, teaches babies how to learn to deal effectively with physiological arousal without being totally dependent on adults.

Learning to sing and learning about my own song

Within the context of attachment relationships, infants start immediately to learn about their sense of self. Winnicott (1973) described how mothers attentively hold their babies during everything they do and how this special contact starts the discovery of a physical self, to be able to physically feel the body as the place wherein one lives. Gergely and Watson (1996) proposed that the process for affect regulation and of emotional self-awareness and control in infancy starts with newborn babies' innate interest in aspects of the environment that forms the basis of a primary representation of the bodily self. In other words, the infant has an ability to pay attention to and recognise aspects of their world that react in response to their actions in a way that perfectly reflects their action or activity. From the outside, for instance, you might see a baby showing fascination for a mobile that moves in response to their leg movement. Again, synchronicity is important, as the infant is sensitive to change in the frequency or intensity of the movement of the mobile, and if there is a delay in movement of the mobile their interest diminishes. The infant might show shock and surprise if a mobile moves more or less than the amount of effort they have put in to moving it.

These experiences are a perfect reflection of self, of an infant's own physical movements, and are particularly important as they are the first indication that an infant seeks to find their sense of self and that there is a mechanism that provides awareness of physical self. Gergely and Watson argue that in the beginning of life the perceptual system is set with a bias to attend to and explore the external world and build representations of experience in this way. In terms of developing a sense of self, of being aware of where you begin and where you end – what is me and what is not me – is a great place to start.

Although infants are skilled communicators, they do not know their psychological selves. Their emotional states are not separated out from one another, their self is unintegrated and experience is fragmented. However, they are able to look outwards, and are interested to find others who can tune into them in order to find their psychological self; they also make sense of themselves in relation to their impact on and interaction with others, which begins much earlier on than previously thought. Gergely and Watson's studies show that, at about three or four months of age, infants become much more interested in aspects of the environment that are near perfect contingencies, for example with a parent who imitates their actions. Within a safe and secure relationship, infants become curious and engage with others who respond to their signs (Trevarthen *et al.* 2011), and so are able to explore faces and the expressions on them. Infants first become sensitised to their emotional states through their parents' 'marked' reflections of their emotion displays during affect-regulative interactions. For example, such an interaction could be the look of excitement on the face of a parent that was a response to seeing their infant wiggle their legs in excitement and anticipation of being picked up. The shift to look outwards to a parent who can tune into the infant's inner world helps the child to become progressively more aware of their inner states; it also coincides with parenting behaviours that switch to take note of and respond to emotionally laden interactions. In this way, we see how an infant needs a parent to tune into their inner world, to imagine what is going on in their mind in subtle but immediately contingent ways. The beginnings of our ability to regulate our emotions come from an attuned parent reading our emotional states, where we are treated as emotional and intentional beings before having the capacity to be truly so.

Because you react to me I can know what I feel (and feel better)

The parent's capacity to mirror effectively their child's internal state is at the heart of affect regulation. Facial and vocal mirroring of affective behaviour is a central feature of parental affective regulative interactions in the first year of life. But how does an infant manage not to attribute their emotional state to their parent and become more worried, angry or excited? After all, when in a state of worry, seeing your parent worry might make you worry more! Importantly, a parent instinctively and automatically marks on their facial expression an exaggerated, slightly different, often softer version of their infant's emotional state (for example, raised eyebrows that express concern and sympathy, as well as the infant's original feeling of sadness). This response to their infant's inner world decouples the emotional display from the parent displaying the emotion, but still is registered by the infant as being strongly related to their inner world. Crucially, this parental response becomes anchored to the infant's own self-state (Gergely and Watson 1996). In other words, internal experiences become represented externally first; they are observable and contribute to self-understanding. Rather than being in and experiencing an emotional state without the awareness of their state of mind, the infant will eventually develop the ability to recognise that they are in an emotional state. This is sometimes referred to as the primary representation of an emotional state moving to a secondary representation (Fonagy *et al.* 2005). This secondary representation provides a cognitive means for accessing and attributing emotional states to self, enabling a child to *have* an emotion rather than *being* that emotion. This process can give distance from the intensity of the emotion.

As marked expressive displays from the parent are a response to the infant, parental responses feel more under the child's control, which increases their sense of agency and has a soothing effect. There is a sense of causal control: 'My parent can see me, is responding to me and is responding because of me.' An infant, at that moment, has been represented in the mind of the parent as an intentional being, their parent's mirroring of behaviour reducing feelings of helplessness as the child comes to understand that their physical self can initiate causal influences in the environment. This has been termed the birth of agentive self (Bateman and Fonagy 2012).

As you tune into me I can tune into myself

Infants become independent subjects only if they are recognised as such, as beings with minds, wills and feelings of their own, by their caregivers. Thus, a sensitive caregiver relates to their baby as a subject long before an infant has any conception of other minds and other subjectivities, let alone his or her own. The mother is treating her child as an intentional being with thoughts and desires long before the child has actually developed these abilities, which is a hallmark of parental reflective functioning and linked to a reflective self (Fonagy and Target 1997). A baby needs caregivers to enter into a relationship with them in order to be able to understand themselves. As a parent helps a baby to find their own emotional states in the parent's face, much as Winnicott described within the earliest primary experience, a baby is able to see the parent's displayed affect as their own, rather than as that of the caregiver's.

How does coherence and integration of experience happen? Before the emergence of self, infants rely totally on seeing themselves in the minds of others; their self only exists in others' minds. The self is only an extension of the experience of the other. We find our mind only in the minds of our parents and, later, other attachment figures thinking about us. As the child and adolescent psychotherapist Margot Waddell stated:

> Psychoanalytically based psychotherapy has, for many years, presented an unwavering and increasingly evidence-based picture of the degree to which the developmental capacities and lasting inner resources of infants and children are shaped, from the first, by the quality – that is the consistency and love – of the earliest relational environment. Initially that means the mother's or primary carer's mind. It is almost a truism that children learn to think by being thought about; that an infant's essential learning about him or herself takes place in the encounter of one mind with another from the very moment of birth. (2002:22)

A mother's representation of a child as an intentional being is communicated in her interactions and the child develops a more abstract understanding of the self. An infant develops a mind because the caregiver has the baby's mind in mind (Fonagy *et al.* 2005). Being able to fit together the puzzle pieces that represent 'me' happens only when a parent can tune in, reflect back and enable the infant's recognition of themselves in the mental state of the parent. It is this process that lies at the root of the sense of personal selfhood. Emotions find a name, and furthermore in a secure relationship, the mother provides a container for these emotional states in a way that helps the infant to regulate them.

When infants and carers enter into emotional experiences, infants begin to learn about their own thoughts, intentions, feelings and beliefs through the parents interacting with them. The inner representation by the infant is part of the core self and comes to be how children see and feel about themselves and how they expect others to feel about them.

Knowing me, knowing relationships

These early relationships with our parents are incredibly important. Research points to the fact that parents' attuned interactions help their children feel safe and valued; this in turn helps them develop the skills needed to bounce back from adversity throughout childhood, adolescence and into adulthood. Being able to utilise the skill of mentalising, to know your own mind and to understand that other people have minds (albeit ones that you cannot directly see into or know for certain), and to rely on others, helps children deal with the external world. To use Winnicott's phrase, 'good enough' experiences help us act and be different in different environments, held together by continuity of memory and identity. However, an infant's reliance on caregivers to accurately reflect back their experiences leaves them emotionally vulnerable, and the impact of this will be discussed later in this chapter.

A bedrock of secure responsive caregiving allows the continuity of emotional security and leads to integration of the self. This capacity to mentalise self and other is a protective factor in an individual's capacity to deal with interpersonal difficulties and to process experiences. Children become able to pick up on what other people are feeling, which acts as a protective function. Good enough experiences act as a buffer during childhood and adolescence; there is a correlation between sensitive parenting and the skills and abilities to negotiate relationships. As mentalisation involves emotional understanding and attunement to the mental states of the self and other (and importantly the separateness and distinctive nature of the minds of self and other), it is also thought to facilitate and enhance the development of interpersonal relationships and social competence (Allen, Fonagy and Bateman 2008). During middle childhood, children make great strides in their mentalising abilities, internalising their parents' ability to mentalise and applying this to increasingly complex emotions and memories (Steele and Steele 2005). Being able to develop mentalisation in this period means children are more able to manage the feelings generated within their peer relationships, because they have learned about the important distinction between their own and other minds, and the different perspectives inherent within them. They can be fun to be with, can have a shared understanding about relationships, manage conflict, and see things from other people's points of view. Children can perceive changes in peers' cues as a trigger to adjust and stay in sync. As such, they are more likely to form meaningful and fulfilling peer relationships.

The importance of peer relationships becomes more marked in adolescents, who will have ongoing relationships with parents that are secure in nature. Where the parent continues to understand that the adolescent has a mind of their own with their own opinions and thoughts, conflict and difference can be respected. Individuals with the capacity to mentalise are less likely to experience an activation of their attachment system while engaged in relationships with other people, as they perceive others to react in a predictably benign and non-threatening manner (George and Solomon 2008). As such, they have a greater amount of free mental space to mentalise within their relationships and be in tune with their partners in adulthood (Fonagy *et al.* 2003).

Our attachment relationships are a mechanism not just for promoting survival from danger or meeting physical needs, but also for promoting our emotional and cognitive survival. Having the skills to mentalise means children can manage their emotional responses, can connect emotionally to others and increase their capacity to process and understand trauma. Without these abilities, as we will see, the chances of being able to process and integrate traumatic experiences are reduced, while the chances of repeated additional and compounding trauma are increased.

Development of a fragmented sense of self in the context of toxic stress and misattuned parenting

Mentalising others is an imaginative process because, as the minds of others are opaque, you can never know for sure what someone else is thinking or feeling. However, under stress, explicit reflective mentalising is superseded by implicit and automatic mentalising, driving careful consideration of others' mental states underground (Fonagy and Luyten 2009). When stressed parents overreact in a situation, they can make quick, automatic judgements about their child. Thus it is normal that, in the course of parenting, a parent will misunderstand their child and the child will get an experience of feeling misunderstood by the parent.

Additionally, a child's parents have their own minds, which can be influenced by many things, including a strong emotion. It can be difficult for a mother or father to respond to their child's needs because of the strength of their emotions in the relationship at that moment. This strong emotion can dictate how a parent interprets and reacts to the child's behaviour. Equally, the ability to respond to an infant or child can be heavily influenced by a distracted state of mind (Cooper and Redfern 2016).

Despite this, and perhaps somewhat surprisingly, there is something helpful about being misunderstood and misunderstanding others in the context of a loving, secure relationship. This gives exposure to live experiences of temporary rupture, which are necessary and normal within the safety of secure relationships. Such happenings bring benefits. For example, a child can learn which behaviours are acceptable, or that other people have differing views and those difficult feelings can be tolerated and contained within relationships. Misunderstandings give exposure to different perspectives, and implicit in this is exposure to the workings of another mind and the mental states inherent within.

In a secure relationship, such ruptures are offset by the bedrock of a great many attuned experiences within which a child has felt valued, seen and safe, and are followed by a quick repair process where the parent takes the initiative to reconnect. Children experience and learn that broken connections can be repaired, and can be followed by feeling very close, safe and connected to a parent who cares and is caring. Feeling safe is vitally important to a child's development. What happens in extreme examples, where minds develop in fear-laden contexts with traumatic caregivers? How does a child's emotional development and sense of self become affected when they are emotionally and physically dependent on a caregiver who inflicts harm and instils fear? What and who can the child rely on to guide their understanding of others' wishes, intentions and feelings when the responses the child receives induce panic, overwhelming terror and abandonment?

When parents cannot tune in

There are differences in the way that some parents interact with their children, which can be particularly disruptive to their development. The Cardiff Child Protection Systematic Review highlighted that parents who struggled to consistently meet their children's emotional needs lacked sensitivity in response to their infant's cues and their own responses were often unpredictable. Mothers often interpreted their babies' cues as being overly demanding and felt irritated when they expressed their needs. This high-risk group was also unresponsive to their infants' cues for help, as well as to changes to their child's facial expressions. In relation to older children, emotionally neglectful parents continued to lack attunement, could be demanding and were less likely to talk to their children about emotional experiences in an appropriate way, which decreased the likelihood of attuned, emotionally responsive interacting.

A mother's tolerance to stress and her ability to stay present with her child are linked to her level of sympathy and perception of distress in her infant. Her perception of her child could be distorted by strong feelings associated with unresolved trauma, despite her ability to understand that her child is an individual with a separate mind (Schechter *et al.* 2006). Trauma interferes with a parent's ability to be present, and to think and respond in a reflective manner rather than with projections, distortions or premature conclusions when considering motives for children's behaviours (Slade 2005).

Researchers have investigated the impact on the relationship between mother and child when synchronicity and timing within interactive sequences are disrupted. Some parents can find it extremely difficult to tune into their young children. As a result, their interactions lose musicality, and their responses lack sensitivity to the feelings and intentionality of their child. A child is less likely to experience these emotional exchanges as being contingent to their state and there is a mismatch of internal state and information from the environment. In the Still Face Test, Tronick and colleagues (1978) demonstrated the marked impact on an infant when a parent does not co-ordinate their responses to their child; the child is not seen psychologically. The infant quickly becomes distressed and dysregulated. Although in the experiment there is repair where the infant experiences the positive and regulating impact of reconnecting with the attuned mother, in neglectful or abusive situations a child may not be given this opportunity. Instead, it is both the abusive behaviour from a parent combined with the lack of reconnection and associated repair that impacts on them.

Attuned relationships are critical to feeling heard, being seen, being valued and feeling safe, and are pivotal for a well-organised functional brain (Perry and Hambrick 2008). If attuned, interactions are like perfectly co-ordinated dances, matched by rhythm and style, whereas chronically misattuned interactions are devastating in their impact and reach, and constitute repeated traumatic experiences. Dancing with a partner who does not see you or sees only what they want to see, or hates dancing with you, is incredibly painful and damaging.

Disharmony and brain development – is there anyone listening?

Children who do not feel safe in infancy have trouble regulating their moods and emotional responses as they grow older (van der Kolk 2014). There is a growing body of evidence that adverse emotional and social experiences in infancy alter the architecture of the brain itself. Instead of the brain developing in an orderly way (Perry and Hambrick 2008), it develops differently because of the impact of stimulation provided by the social and emotional environment in which a child grows up. Attuned parenting, as described earlier in this chapter, builds a functional, efficient brain. Secure attachment promotes neural connections, helping to strengthen and integrate key brain structures (Stein and Kendall 2004:8). However, advances in imaging techniques repeatedly show that a child raised in an abusive and/or neglectful home has marked differences in organisation and neurological connectedness (Teicher *et al.* 2003).

Research has shown that the most damaging qualities were shown by those parents who emotionally distanced themselves when they felt rejected by their children (Lyons-Ruth *et al.* 2006). They were more likely to become distant when their needs were not met, and found it hard to take an adult position in the relationship. Not able to separate their own needs from those of their children resulted in mothers becoming helpless and sullen, unresponsive and hurt when their children did not dance to their tune. The normal breaking away of infants in an interaction for some parents can represent a more malign intention, that of rejection or personal attack, and can lead to withdrawal and disconnection as a parent retreats in an experience of hurt. A traumatised infant does not have the same opportunities for socio-emotional learning during critical periods of right-brain development as children in healthy homes. Without a sympathetic response and used to a parent who ignores their needs, the child anticipates rejection and withdrawal and blocks these experiences in an attempt to become disconnected from them. Misattunement and disengagement of a parent during an infant's childhood is shown to be a predictor of dissociative symptoms found in early adulthood. When children do not learn to feel safe, they develop an impaired sense of inner reality, dissociation and loss of self-regulation. Infants who are not truly seen or known by their mothers can become adults who cannot know or see.

Is that really my song?

If accurate and contingent emotional responses help infants work out differences between their self-states, which then become the foundations of a core self, it is little wonder that inaccurate mirroring and biased attributions on the part of the parent leads the child to develop a distorted mental organisation. When an infant interacts in the environment, what instead might be reflected back to them? What happens when what is reflected back has little link to their self-state? For example, what happens when the infant's inner state is really anxiety and fear, but what is reflected back is aggression and anger from a parent who feels persecuted by the infant? How can this mismatch become incorporated into a sense of self?

In the case of mirroring which is non-contingent and in the absence of an authentic basis for selfhood, the infant uses the available stimuli instead, leading to an insecure sense of self. The internalisation of this mismatched mirroring response will likely generate an internal experience that contributes to a fragmented sense of self, a sense of self that is not coherent or fully known and experienced.

Incongruence between what an infant might feel and the reflected affect from the parent distorts the child's self-understanding and leads to the development of what has been called the alien self (Fonagy 2000). The alien self can be seen as having much in common with Winnicott's (1965) concept of false self. The alien self develops over time when many misattuned responses from the parent, which are not congruent but hostile, are internalised by an infant and are experienced as if belonging to someone else. They are felt as being alien, crucially because they do not fit with the infant's felt experience. The child internalises the mental state of victimiser, into the alien part of self, but can then feel oppressed and persecuted by this hostile being, that is at once the child but not the child. Ultimately, the child can experience their own mind as torturing them, as it represents an internalised other, out of kilter with their inner emotional self, creating a sense of confusion about the emotion and severe disruption of the ability to regulate the emotion. This dysregulated emotion then overwhelms the child.

> Charlie felt a sense of relief from being persecuted from within himself, either in the form of self-destructive behaviours like self-harm, but also by externalising the alien part of himself into others. He felt harshly criticised by staff, perceiving their hatred towards him. By externalising these feelings on to others he felt persecuted from the outside instead of from the inside by the staff treating him or family members, giving rise to coherence and energy against a persecutor. He felt organised from within.

Distortions in representation of self and self-organisation result from dysfunctional attachment relationships, and if a mother is not able to meet her baby's impulses and needs, as Winnicott described, the baby instead becomes the mother's idea of what the baby is (van der Kolk 2014). If maternal care is not good enough then the infant does not really come into their own existence. Since there is no continuity in being, their personality instead is built on the basis of reactions that have no relationship to their inner states. Experiencing childhood trauma perpetuates difficulty expressing and modulating emotions, and changes to one's self-perception, which may include a sense of self impacted by shame, guilt and low self-worth. Failure to find the self in a caregiver can profoundly distort how children experience their inner world. Children can become vulnerable to shutting down direct feedback from their bodies as they discount inner sensations to try and adjust to caregiver needs. Feelings and associated sensations are shut out from experience as the children perceive something is wrong. The conclusion is the abuse was their fault and they expect further abuse, which paves the way for the possibility of a perpetual cycle of trauma.

Shutting out terrifying tunes

Parents of securely attached children promote and prompt their children to safely explore and reflect on their mental states. This brings meaning to the activity (Cooper and Redfern 2016) and encourages children to think about their own internal states; it becomes a fruitful exercise. When a child has a terrifying parent (or one whose mind is extremely hard to understand) in families where abuse and fear proliferate, self-reflection is discouraged. This, then, impedes the development of self-agency. Children who experienced maltreatment may have learned to inhibit their mentalising function, or may not have developed the capacity to mentalise due to the trauma they experienced to their attachment system (Allen and Fonagy 2006). When children have been so brutalised and traumatised and then spend so much time burying the residual terror and panic somewhere because they cannot tolerate knowing, they also cannot understand that their anger, terror or collapse has anything to do with that experience. They don't talk; they act and deal with feelings by being enraged, shut down, compliant or defiant. This was most forcefully described to me by Jude.

Jude was an intelligent 17-year-old who came into therapy feeling dissatisfied and angry at past mental health support. She was resolute, in the first session, that her past had no bearing on her functioning and that she would fight both physically and psychologically to resist any of my attempts to explore it. I was constantly impressed by the fact that she attended any sessions at all, as they may easily have represented a terrifying experience. The experience of being with someone who was truly interested in her must have generated a deep mistrust that I would probe and uncover terrifying, uncontainable terror, which only expressed itself in the form of dissociative episodes and flashbacks.

Carrying memories of feeling safe growing up with their parents is a luxury some children do not have. If you have no memory of safety, you cannot easily turn to others and ask for help in an appropriate way. So, when you find your mind so terrifyingly overwhelming, you are truly stuck between two sources of significant threat: your own mind or the untrustworthy other.

In order to know who we are, to have a stable identity, we must know and feel what is and what is not real, to trust our memories and tell them apart from imagination. Dissociation in adulthood is linked strongly to abandonment, helplessness and disconnection in childhood. Erasing awareness might be of upmost importance when you are young and living in terrifying times, but you may end up not knowing your own mind.

> Jude could feel very passionate about other people's causes but she often did not know what she really thought or felt about herself and her own life. She would become really concerned that she did not know who she was, that fundamentally she could not seem to grasp a sense of her genuine self. Her experience was much, much more than the sense that other people perhaps might have, for example playing a role at college or with certain friends and being different around parents. Jude felt this in a more profound sense, where she was unable to fall back on a core sense of who she was, and she hated herself for it. The price she paid for blocking out awareness was a sensation of being fake and of being unable to connect to others and that others could not truly know her. She could feel utterly alone, feeling empty and worthless, which was unbearable. These were often the times when I felt she was most at risk.

I can't tune into others

Research has shown that children who have been physically abused interpret and understand emotional signals in facial expressions differently from children who have not been abused (Pollak *et al.* 2000).

Children, at a perceptual level, overrate anger and aggression in faces, seeing danger and threat where there is little evidence of these things. McCrory *et al.* (2013) showed through an ingenious research paradigm that maltreated children had heightened neural responsiveness to heightened emotion in faces in general (not just threat based) in the early pre-conscious stages of processing, i.e. before the influence of higher order systems. Such studies help us understand the impact of implicit automatic reflexive mentalising, which relies on implicit maps to guide interpretations of the world. In attachment situations and stressful situations such implicit mentalising predominates and guides interaction, so if your map is one of abuse and maltreatment, this is what you rely on to automatically interpret others' behaviour.

The developmental period of middle childhood, where school-age children are putting into practice their acquired skills of mentalising, is disrupted for children who experience or have experienced childhood trauma. This is because they cope by avoiding thinking about the mind and mental states of their caregiver to protect the self (Fonagy *et al.* 1996). Instead of middle childhood becoming a period of great change, their defensive disruption of the capacity to depict feelings and thoughts in themselves and others creates a vulnerability to interpersonal stress (Fonagy *et al.* 1994). Children have an impaired capacity to mentalise, and during implicit reflexive mentalising individuals may fall back on negative and abusive default positions. This means they are at huge risk of ongoing rejection. Without practising social skills and thinking reflectively about others, they may lack the subtle skills of accurately inferring shifts in the mental states of others and being able to tolerate and stay present during interpersonal difficulties. Instead, they may numb out and become distant, or conversely overreact and reject others. These abilities are important to help build up a network of reliable friends, since without them, peers can find them odd, somehow different, distant, hostile or unreasonable, which leads to further rejection.

Sarah was an 11-year-old girl whose inability to focus and learn was a cause for concern for her school. I observed her in the playground waiting in line. Her peers stood away from her and formed a corridor a foot distance either side of her in the line. They whispered jokes behind her back and dared each other to touch her. From the outside at least, she seemed oblivious to what was going on. However, when I had the privilege to work with her some years later, she remembered the isolation and disconnection she had from her peers throughout primary and the majority of secondary school, and how puzzling she found others. Shortly after my school visit, Sarah had the courage to confide in a very trusted adult the extent of the heinous abuse she suffered as a young child, and her difficulties concentrating could be put into the context of the effects of chronic, terrifying interpersonal trauma.

Normal developmental shifts in adolescence include the propensity to hypermentalise about peers and to experience emotions more acutely. When individuals with a poorly integrated sense of self reach adolescence, they are poorly equipped with the skills and resources to manage and think through what they want, think or feel. Without the continuity of self, life is at risk of being experienced as a series of fragmented action episodes, full of risky, chaotic and traumatic events. There is no interest or inclination to bring it all together to reflect, discuss and explore with others and learn from the process.

Jude felt that her emotions were something to be avoided and that she had no agency over them. They ran her life. It was very hard for Jude to start to contemplate a process of learning from them or to think about what happened in interpersonal exchanges. She could feel powerless to prevent emotional torrents, was terrified to contemplate her own mind. It upset her to reflect on what happened in interpersonal exchanges, as often she would not recognise the 17-year-old who had reacted in the way that she had. Reflecting on past interactions only represented, in her mind, her failure.

Conclusion

Recent advances in neuroscience and the integration with psychological and developmental understanding have revealed insights into how early experiences influence fundamental mental processes. These include emotional regulation and memory and offer new ways of explaining the link between childhood maltreatment and psychiatric disorder (McCrory and Viding 2015). These advances deepen our understanding of human experience and highlight the sustained impact on children who have had to endure, and survive, physically and chronically abusive parents.

Helping children who have endured such experiences requires a good understanding of the difficulties they face, and an incredibly emotionally resilient therapeutic environment, consisting of both a team and individuals who can show interest, curiosity and motivation to attune and start to bring harmony and integration to the child's life.

CHAPTER 2

UNINTEGRATION AND ATTACHMENT

The Legacy of Bowlby and Winnicott

Christine Bradley

Introduction

Our understanding about attachment theory has developed over the past 50 years, with extensive research evidencing conceptual thinking on the subject. One of the key themes is that of maternal deprivation and the continual disruption of the attachment relationship between the infant and primary carer. An insecure attachment results in long-term cognitive, social and emotional difficulties throughout the child's development and into adulthood. The purpose of this chapter is to review the legacy of John Bowlby and Donald Winnicott, integrating their theory and practice skills into contemporary thinking. It aims to help readers to recognise that it is possible to repair the emotional damage in infants and young children whose breakdown of early attachment relationships has interrupted their development and personal integration. As well as the legacy of Bowlby and Winnicott, there will also be a link between their concepts and emerging research from neuroscience. This link helps the concepts move forward with a greater understanding about the biological and psychological development of children and young people.

Child psychiatrist and psychoanalyst John Bowlby defined attachment theory during the 1960s as a conceptual framework that provided a secure base for the grounding of children's emotional development. During this period, Donald Winnicott formulated his theory of emotional integration and unintegration, presenting these as the precursor to attachment theory. He held the view that attachment theory was framed by a transition from absolute dependency on the primary carer who was in a state of primary and maternal preoccupation with them, through to interdependency, with the two people interacting together. This enabled the infant to attach to the primary carer and create the foundation for a secure base from which they could develop their sense of self and individuality.

In explaining the earliest emotional state that exists between the primary carer and infant, Winnicott (1978:99) wrote, 'There is no such thing as a baby, a baby only feels they exist when they experience themselves as a part of their primary carer.' He observed that the primary carer and infant had to experience being a single entity, connected physically and psychologically through their 'primary merger'. This feeling is internalised and enables the infant to begin their developmental journey.

However, when we are working with children who are struggling with the breakdown of an attachment relationship, or who are floundering in an unintegrated state because there is no emotional beginning, we constantly need to ask: What exactly is needed for repair and recovery to take place? How do we repair the damage done to children and young people, which has had an impact on their maturational and emotional development, leaving them unable to manage themselves in age-appropriate ways? Often, this is because their inner world is consumed with feelings of panic, rage and unbearable anxieties which cannot be thought about. In the language of neuroscience, they are unable to regulate their emotions. Such powerful emotions relate back to their early experiences of trauma, hostility and abandonment, which have become deeply embedded in their minds. This embodiment in the mind is what Bowlby referred to as an 'internal working model'. Where children's feelings are too overwhelming for them to manage, it can result in destructive and self-destructive behaviour being acted out by them. The repetitive nature and difficulty of dealing with these unmanageable and unthinkable emotions can become too powerful and difficult for their carers and workers to contain emotionally. The result is that often their placements with family, foster or children's homes break down and the cycle of repeated trauma, abuse and abandonment continues. If we are to prevent this cycle from continuing, as carers and workers we need to find the starting point from which their care and treatment can begin. As Dockar-Drysdale said in terms of provision of primary experience, we need to 'return to the point of failure' (1990:169).

Meeting with Donald Winnicott

I met Dr Donald Winnicott in 1970, when as a young graduate I had just started work at the Cotswold Community. For two years before my arrival, the Cotswold School, as it was previously known, had been going through a transition from an approved school (known today as a young offenders' institution) into a therapeutic community for adolescent boys. When I arrived, the culture was moving from one of harsh, institutional warehousing into one that was becoming more focused on meeting children's needs from a stronger and more insightful therapeutic approach.

Donald Winnicott was a celebrated paediatrician and psychoanalyst who visited the Community periodically to offer advice to the senior workers and managers. At that time, I was working with a very difficult 15-year-old boy (Paul) through play, where he was making a model village with my help. One day the village would be alive, trees growing, shops open and people talking to each other. The following day, the trees would have died, shops closed and nobody living there. Intuitively, I felt he wanted to communicate something important, but I could not grasp what. I spoke with our staff consultant, Barbara Dockar-Drysdale, who, after listening to my anxieties about the work I was undertaking with Paul, responded to me, 'You must speak to Donald, he is visiting next week.' I was in awe at the thought of meeting Donald Winnicott and showing him my work. I was young and inexperienced; he was a highly respected icon in the field of child development and psychotherapy. The following week came and I met him and took him to the playroom, showing him the model village. I said to him, 'You see Dr Winnicott, I do not understand what Paul is trying to say to me.' He stared at the village intensely for some time, while I was waiting for what I thought would be the insight of the century! After a few moments, he looked at me and said, 'Do you know my dear, neither do I.' He then continued, 'But Christine, carry on not knowing and one day the real knowing will come through to you. When it does, it will be a knowing with meaning and sincerity. If one feels they have to know all the time, often they do not know at all. So, my dear, carry on not knowing.'

I followed his advice and indeed, in time came, to understand that on the days Paul felt so dead inside himself, the village had to come to an end. I began to help him through the emotions that made him feel dead when the village closed, helping him to bring the village and himself back to life again. Of course, as Winnicott had implied, because we worked this out together it had great meaning for both Paul and myself. Sadly, Winnicott died the following year, his advice becoming the legacy he left me which has lived on, and proved to be right in both my professional and personal life. Acquiring the belief and trust in ourselves to be able to live through a stage of 'not knowing' before reaching the important element of 'knowing' can be a difficult and painful time for us all. It is especially important in work with children who have suffered so much that they have not been able to comprehend. These children are on the one hand full of confusion and chaos and on the other want a magical quick fix. Carers and workers need to be able to manage their own sense of not knowing if they are to help children and young people feel better about themselves. The work is slow and often painful. When we are managing the reality and uncertainties of external factors, we need to have a philosophical underpinning which makes it bearable and manageable for us all.

Bowlby and Winnicott: the legacy

Although there were differences between the work of Bowlby and Winnicott, they shared an important belief about the mother–infant relationship. Their view was that the earliest relationship between mother and infant profoundly affected the emotional well-being and developing sense of self in the infant. This provides the groundwork for their ongoing maturational development in later years. Despite the similarities and divergences between their thinking, it should be recognised that they were both intellectually and psychologically committed to investigating the importance of the mother–infant relationship as providing a secure base, sense of self and individuality in the infant and small child.

Hunter (1991), in Hauptmann and Reeves (2005:170), observed:

It has become commonplace to regard Bowlby and Winnicott as having essentially the same view about early separation from the mother as a contributory factor in a variety of disturbances in childhood, social and psychological development including notably juvenile delinquency. This near-identity was given near the end of Bowlby's life, in which he declared, 'I always held the view that Winnicott and I were singing the same tune. We were essentially giving the same message, but again he didn't like my theoretical ideas.'

Although their theories emerged from the mother–child relationship, their contributions to the field took different turns. Bowlby was primarily a scientist using research-based evidence to underpin the importance of attachment theory. Winnicott in contrast was rooted in a more subjective way of thinking that was creative and playful. Both held a deep and sincere admiration for each other's work, while recognising and accepting their differences.

Fonagy (2001:102) wrote, 'It is now widely recognised that the formulation of their theories are compatible with each other.' Although Bowlby did not ignore the internal world, he tried to reformulate aspects of psychoanalytical thinking, turning his attention to more environmentally observable aspects of human behaviour. Winnicott's thinking was more subtle, complex, imaginative, wide ranging and flexible (Hauptmann and Reeves 2005). He describes the concept of an infant's journey from unintegration through to emotional integration, as being necessary to be achieved, if a healthy attachment relationship between the mother and infant is to develop, which in turn aids further maturational development (Winnicott 1965).

Figure 2.1 presents a comparison of the work of Bowlby and Winnicott.

Bowlby: Attachment

A secure base as a grounding point for emotional development and attachment relationships to begin.

Winnicott: Emotional integration

Feeling whole and complete as a person with a sense of self; exhibits empathy and remorse; has evolved defence mechanisms to protect self from stress; values meaningful relationships: can share the world with others.

Attachment disorders

These arise where the secure base breaks down as a result of trauma and results in the following behaviours:

- Avoidant/resistant/helpless/hostile
- Disorganised/controlling
- Dysregulated
- Avoidant/ambivalent
- Resistant/dependent.

These prevent the development of healthy and secure attachment relationships.

Fragile integration

Has the beginnings of a sense of self but feels vulnerable at times. Coming together as a person but still very fragile and can easily break down when confronted with stressful situations. Reality is still difficult to manage and needs emotional support.

The beginning of transition from absolute dependence to relative dependence where the individual begins to relate to others outside the primary carer.

Pre-attachment

Pre-attachment related to the first three months of life.

Where the secure base is formed through the mother–infant bonding, the infant feels emotionally contained and bonded with her.

Where bonding does not take place within the first six months, it directly impacts on the maturation of healthy human growth and development, the infant's sense of self and their ability to fulfil their potential.

At times can regress to infantile states.

Unintegration

Little or no sense of self; feels emotionally isolated or seeks to merge with others.

Does not feel held in mind or emotionally contained.

No sense of absolute dependence with their primary carer; fear of emotional and physical abandonment more powerful than a sense of emotional holding.

Anxieties are more primitive, with no boundaries between fantasy and reality; inability to learn from experience; a tendency to recreate destructive or self-destructive behaviours; overwhelmed with panic, rage and unthinkable anxiety.

Figure 2.1: A comparison between Bowlby and Winnicott

John Bowlby

The prime focus of John Bowlby's work was a secure base for the infant and small child as a grounding point for their emotional development. He emphasised that children's experiences of interpersonal relationships were crucial to their psychological development. His research-based evidence, and experience of working with the World Health Organization on the mental health of homeless children, meant that his work was framed by a social policy ethic, while also relating to the internal and external world experiences of children. His thinking and work was based on psychological, sociological and social policy perspectives, taking a global view on the nature of human development. Howe (2011b:184) observed that 'under the creative genius of John Bowlby, insights garnered from evolutionary theory, ethology, systems theory and developmental psychology were fashioned over a number of years into what is today known as attachment theory'.

Bowlby's compassionate and logical thinking, which he applied to his research and writing about attachment, has stood the test of time. Howe (2011a:196) notes:

> attachment theory offers a compelling set of ideas about children, developing close relationships with their main caregivers. They describe how they attempt to adapt and survive in their particular caregiving environment, and how their behaviours and coping strategies can be understood as functional within the caregiving setting which gave rise to them.

The key focus of attachment theory from the beginning has been that of the importance of creating a secure base for the infant and small child through the attachment relationship with their mother or primary carer. The three prime aims for an infant who has achieved a secure attachment relationship with their primary carer in the early stages of their maturational development are as follows:

- Regulation: managing and containing emotions and behaviour.

- Mentalisation: beginning to think about their actions and learn from their experiences.

- Activation: acquiring mental and physical energy which leads them into exploratory behaviour, including playing and learning.

A child with a secure base who is able to take in their experiences of the outside world is more capable of communicating emotions to a primary caregiver during the process of separation when feeling distressed. Provided they receive care and support from their carer, the infant is able to build up their defences, and think about their behaviour and the effect that it has on others, as the mentalisation process begins. This process can support their developing self to explore and test out the challenges of the outside world and has an impact on psychological, social and behavioural development.

There are a number of expressions of attachment disorder (see Figure 2.1 earlier), with disorganised attachment being seen as a subgroup of insecure attachment. Since Bowlby began his work and research developing the concept of attachment theory, the two dimensions of attachment relationships between infant, child and caregiver – secure and insecure – remain the same as he described them:

> Secure attachment: securely attached children have received sensitive, psychologically minded caregiving which has a positive effect on their psychosocial development. They sense that at times of need, their caregivers are available and sensitively responsive. They develop deep feelings of trust when they become distressed and are soothed and comforted quickly by their caregivers. (Howe 2011a:188)

> Insecure attachment: for insecure children, caregivers are less optimally sensitive, psychologically available and responsive to their emotional needs. The caregiver's inability to 'mentalise' and hold the infant or child in their mind will affect their children's attachment organisation and subsequent psychosocial development. Their internal working model and sense of self is less positive than the experiences of the child who is securely attached. (Howe 2011a:190)

While the quality of thinking and depth of knowledge about the nature of attachment theory both psychologically and biologically has increased considerably over the past 40–50 years, Bowlby's pattern of thinking has continued, such is his legacy.

However, workers and carers of infants, children and young people must be careful not to use the theory as a way of defending themselves from the panic, rage and unthinkable anxieties that are embedded in the emotional lives of those for whom they are responsible. Carers need to understand and respond to the child's emotional needs rather than reacting to their behaviour. The following case example will illustrate how easy it is to use diagnostic concepts as a defence against the worker's anxieties when they are having to discover ways of managing the behaviour of emotionally distressed and damaged children and young people.

> Some years ago, I was visiting a children's home to whom I was a consultant. A 13-year-old girl, Ann, had just arrived and was planning to run away, just as she had done from several previous placements in foster families, children's homes and secure unit accommodation. I introduced myself to her and explained why I was visiting – that my work was to help those who were caring for her and the other young people in the home, how to understand them and help them to feel better about themselves. At this point Ann said to me, 'Well, you see, my problem is that I have got an attachment disorder.' I looked rather surprised, and she said, 'My psychiatrist told me; in fact I have the report.' I replied, 'Well, you may have an attachment disorder, but we need to understand how that disorder came about.' She came back with: 'Well, you see, my brother died when he was very little, and so was I. My mother neglected me and could not look after me properly, so I was moved from home to home because nobody could take care of me properly and I was really horrible to them.' I said to her, 'Then it is not at all surprising that you have developed an attachment disorder. You have experienced a great amount of pain, sadness and hurt in your life, and we need to try to make you feel better about what happened to you, helping you to feel more comfortable with where you are now.' Finally, she said surprisingly, 'Why has nobody told me that before?' My final response to her was that I did not know why, but it was never too late to start thinking about 'why you have felt so awful throughout your life, and we need to be helping you to feel better about yourself'.
>
> Using the need assessment and treatment programme that I adapted, the children's home did provide Ann with the care and treatment she required, although she did go through some very turbulent and difficult periods during her daily experiences. Over time she began to express her emotions through story writing, using her creativity to function more positively. Eventually, Ann began to enjoy flower arranging and spoke of becoming a florist. She had begun to view a life for herself which she could believe in and from which she could emotionally develop.

While it is crucial for workers to have a theoretical basis to underpin knowledge about their work, it is equally important that they develop an insight and understanding about their practice skills. It is this combination of theory and practice that will support their work with children who need their help, care and treatment, to commence the journey of recovery from the emotional breakdown and traumatic experiences of their early life. Enabling the child to develop confidence in themselves and to believe that with support they can manage the challenges of the external realities, without becoming overwhelmed by the internal factors they are carrying, mainly depends on skilled therapeutic practice. To make this work, there must be a bridge built between the two worlds of theory and practice, together with a pathway where one side can be reached by the other. Finding the starting point for good therapeutic practice is fundamental to devising therapeutic care and treatment.

Donald Winnicott

Figure 2.2 below sets out the characteristics of unintegration through to integration.

Unintegrated child	Fragile integration	Transition into integration	Integration
No sense of self; consumed by panic, rage and unthinkable anxiety; easily feels persecuted by the outside world and attacks back.	The infant has a brief, positive early experience; however, a breakdown occurs in the relationship before the infant is ready to make the transition. This results in them becoming emotionally fragile, and more susceptible to emotional breakdown at points of anxiety and stress.	Is more creative and can communicate both symbolically and verbally with appropriate support.	Maintains an evolving balance between the inner world and the external world.
The infant does not have an early experience of being held emotionally and as a consequence experiences emotional isolation and a need to merge with others.	Has lengthier periods of functioning than an integrated child.	A developing individual with a stronger sense of self, beginning to learn from experiences. However, the child is vulnerable to early anxiety.	Can express ambivalence; communicate their emotions to others; and relate to others in a group setting.

Figure 2.2: The process from unintegration to integration

Unintegration

Bowlby's focus for developing attachment theory lay in understanding the difference between secure and insecure attachment relationships, which he presented as his foundation stone for the continuing work. Winnicott's main contribution lay in identifying the stages from absolute dependence to independence as a move from unintegration through to integration. He defined this concept as the starting point for the emotional development of children and young people, as they come together as a whole person and learn to manage their relationship with the external world. Hauptmann and Reeves (2005:136) wrote that Winnicott stated, 'Concepts can never be presented to me merely, they must be knitted into the structure of living and being, and this can only be done through my own activity.' Winnicott believed that, during their emotional development, children have a basic desire to be understood. He also believed that children needed to reach a stage where they became an individual in their own right. His point of view was:

> A tiny human being comes into the world endowed with the power to organise his world, a world which she is going to have to face to make their own. This world is presented to her by the environment she is a part of. (Dethiville 2008:7)

Winnicott also stated that if the developing infant was to develop a sense of self they could live with and feel enriched by, it was play and creativity that helped the infant discover the balance between fantasy and reality. This needed to be understood and recognised by those caring for and nurturing them. Winnicott's concept and insight flowed more from a level of subjectivity and creative thinking than Bowlby's, as Bowlby had a more scientific approach. Yet we have come to understand that we need to be able to think at both an objective and subjective level if we are to gain some insight and understanding when meeting and adapting to the emotional needs of children and young people.

Winnicott (1978:41) described 'maternal pre-occupation' as two people (infant and mother) being 'one' for a period, during which time the high level of their emotional needs and demands is met prior to differentiation into a separate personal self. This helps the infant to progressively develop from 'floundering' in their 'unintegrated' state to feeling more whole and complete, working through to a gradual separation from their mother or primary carer and beginning to attach to other people. Trowell observed:

> Winnicott used this term to describe the internal state of the infant –
> that is a state of not being integrated as a person who could develop
> a sense of self, becoming able to experience anxiety. (2011:257)

During the same period the child's brain is developing. More recently Perry (1996:1) noted that 'physical connections between neurons – synaptic connections – did increase and strengthen through repetition', whereas children who did not feel held in the mind of their carer remain emotionally unintegrated and their brain 'can wither through disuse'. As the brain organises, the infant's sense of self, their thinking and emotions, begin to link together, bringing together thinking and feeling.

Usually with 'good enough' provision of maternal preoccupation an infant becomes fragilely integrated towards the first year of life. Where the infant's experience is not good enough, their development will be delayed and they may remain unintegrated. Where the lack of maternal preoccupation is compounded with emotions of hostility and resentment projected onto the infant, the developmental difficulty may be severe. The infant internalises a sense of annihilation, which is unable to be thought about like a thoughtless terror. As a result, the infant has little or no sense of a self who is living and developing as an individual. Instead the infant becomes overwhelmed with feelings of panic, rage and unthinkable anxiety, which cannot be thought about or communicated verbally or non-verbally. The stress of managing their own emotions and relationship with external reality becomes unbearable. As this heightened state is not sustainable, the infant may unconsciously shut down to block out feelings of pain. Sadly, at the same time the infant becomes switched off from all feeling or 'frozen', as Dockar-Drysdale (1958) named this state. Levels of functioning break down as they cease to function. They become withdrawn and cut off from the outside world, or act out in the external environment destructively and self-destructively, with adverse results. Both withdrawal and excessive acting out are attempts to gain some form of control in a frightening and harsh world where little or no comfort can be expected.

In later development, the child finds the intimacy of attaching to another person difficult, sometimes impossible, to achieve. The breakdown of their primary relationships led them to believe that there was no emotional beginning in their life. To survive their unbearable feelings that could not be thought about, they may develop what Winnicott (1978:147) called a 'false self', from which they present themselves as charming and compliant. However, when feeling threatened, the child can very easily become overwhelmed by panic, rage and unthinkable anxiety, leading to violent and unpredictable outbursts, which seem completely at odds with the previous pleasant behaviour. Following the outburst, the child may have no memory of it. Such a child finds it difficult to learn from their experiences. They are disconnected from their own experiences as a way of protecting themselves from pain.

Unintegrated children can be identified through the following aspects of how they respond to ordinary daily events:

- They are constantly seeking for the primary merger which they missed out on as an infant. Because of this it can leave them in danger of identifying with the most difficult and boundary-less parts of other young people, merging and over-identifying with the destructive aspects of their personality. At this stage it is too difficult for them to manage the intimacy of a healthy attachment in their relationships. This type of emotional merger between two or more young children can become very dangerous, as all sense of a personal boundary and self-preservation is lost.

- They can very easily feel persecuted by the outside world and attack accordingly out of revenge. Their internal and external worlds feel at war with each other.

- The depth of their hidden and locked-away feelings of panic, rage, rejection and fear of abandonment can tap into some very difficult feelings in those responsible for them. If the workers 'react' to the children's emotional needs rather than 'respond' in a more thoughtful way, difficulties can quickly escalate with serious consequences.

- It is difficult for them to internalise any good experiences they have been provided with. They do not feel they deserve anything which is good and cannot easily hold onto the sense that anything good has happened. If they can experience something good the unintegrated child often 'spoils' it, before someone else can take it away from them. This way the child protects themselves from further loss. (Bradley 2010:6–7)

It is important to acknowledge that, with unintegrated children, it is always possible for workers to support a healing process, finding the starting point from which they can gain some recovery from their traumas. Before the traumatic experiences can even be considered, the child must first feel safe. This is painstaking work and can take months, if not years. Following this, the focus will need to be on filling some of the developmental gaps through the provision of positive new experiences, so that the child is gradually able to build their inner resources. Through this stage of their life in an environment which can reach out to the lost part of their inner lives, the child may reach a creative way forward in their future development. However, to acquire a stronger sense of self, they do need therapeutic management. Dockar-Drysdale (1990:7) wrote:

> Good child care is not the same as the preoccupation of the ordinary devoted mother, and therapeutic management is again different, although having much in common with primary maternal preoccupation. Where unintegrated children are concerned, there must be involvement.

Good child care is geared into the everyday needs of the child or young person, while therapeutic management also tunes into the emotional needs of the child. Such tuning-in could take the place of the maternal preoccupation, which they did not experience as a small child. The management of the child is based on an understanding of the child's needs and the meaning of their behaviour.

Emotional integration

Winnicott states that infants whose early primary experiences gave them a strong sense of emotional containment and maternal preoccupation from their primary carer felt more enriched by their internal world and had a stronger sense of 'being a person'. However, the child still requires a great amount of support and care if positive development is to continue. Though all development can include turbulent and difficult periods, an integrated child is usually able to work through these with support. As the child begins to develop emotionally, physically and psychologically, they also start to look at and view the outside world as an experience that they can begin to explore. They no longer need the intensely strong continuous and emotional experience they had when they were in a state of a primary merger with their mother or primary carer, which was the centre of their life. They move towards the transitional stage of discovering their own identity and sense of self, because their need for absolute dependency in their relationship with their carer has been met. The infant is now ready to tackle the challenges of the external reality, and attach to others. With continuing support from their primary carer, they start to gain a sense of themselves as individuals.

As the child begins to move away from the period of being at one with another person (primary merger), they begin to come together as an individual with their own sense of self (emotional integration). Emotional integration is characterised by the child being able to:

- share the world with others and keep to the rules

- take part in group activities and to be creative in activities

- attach to others, engaging in meaningful relationships with others and making friendship with peers

- regulate emotions, anxieties, anger and stress

- express feelings when under stress in the external world, learning from experience.

The three stages of dependency needs in the maturational growth and development of children and young people are described below.

ABSOLUTE DEPENDENCE

Absolute dependence represents the early symbiotic relationship between the infant and the carer whereby the maternal preoccupation of the mother is to give the infant a sense of emotional containment and holding. At this stage, if the primary needs are understood and provided for by the primary carer, the infant begins to develop a sense of being a person – a 'self'. Abram explains the infant's vulnerability at this very early stage of brain development:

> In this state, the infant has no means of knowing about the maternal care. He cannot gain control over what is well, and what is badly done, but is only in a position to gain profit or to suffer disturbance. Here conditions that fail do in fact traumatize. (1996:120)

RELATIVE DEPENDENCE

Relative dependence was defined by Winnicott (1978:45) as the first 'not me' situation. The infant is ready to begin to separate from the primary merger with the primary carer. Playing with a toy can become an object which the infant uses to relate to as they begin to separate from their mother primary carer (transitional object). The infant and small child moves towards individuation and begins to play with others. Socialisation and mentalisation become a part of moving towards emotional integration. The infant experiments with independence but needs to re-experience dependence periodically.

INTERDEPENDENCE

The stage of interdependence refers to the evolving independence of the infant or small child where they begin to develop means for 'doing without' actual care. They are now in a position, because their primary needs have been met and their brain is developing, to accumulate memories of care. They start to express themselves and show emotions, and as they begin to think about and learn from these they are able to move towards becoming emotionally fragile and will require additional emotional support from their carers. Winnicott states how failure to meet the infant's needs is especially significant when this happens early in the infant's development:

> The earlier the failure of the environment the more disastrous the outcome for the individual's mental health. If the infant's needs are met during the early precarious states of emotional development he will be in a stronger position to survive environmental failure later on. (Abram 1996:122)

However, Winnicott also acknowledged that it is possible through therapeutic treatment to heal the emotional damage, and give the children and young people a starting point for their developmental growth. These are two very important aspects of the work which need to be included in treatment.

This chapter has discussed that the construct of the sense of self in the infant and young child is the foundation for further maturational growth and development, and a prerequisite for the formation of ego-development and emotional integration.

The management and provision of good therapeutic child care in a well-structured and thoughtful environment can help the child to move from a level of unintegration towards the state of emotional integration. The child can then begin to manage the challenge of meeting the external expectations with support from their carers. Their sense of self should strengthen and maturation occurs as the lost small child in their inner world feels more whole, as a person in their own right, although life will be full of emotional 'ups' and 'downs' which need to be endured when they are managing challenging aspects of internal and external reality. To have reached a level of emotional integration where they can start attaching to other people means that the child has acquired the emotional resources to work through and manage the difficult periods in their life. They value the more positive experiences and see them as meaningful and real.

In his book *Playing and Reality* (1968:2–3) Winnicott wrote:

> Of every individual who has reached the stage of being a unit with a limiting membrane and an outside and an inside, it can be said that there is an inner reality to that individual, an inner world that can be rich or poor and can be at peace or in a state of war. This helps, but is it enough?

He continues to raise a sign of hope for those who arrive at a maturational stage of their life in a state of impoverishment, living their life from an empty shell that has no emotional beginning or starting point, observing:

> One has to allow for the possibility that there cannot be a complete destruction of a human individual's capacity for creative living and that, even in the most extreme cases of compliance and the establishment of a false personality, hidden away somewhere there exists a secret life that is satisfactory because of it being creative or original to that human being. Its unsatisfactoriness must be measured in terms of its being hidden, its lack of enrichment through living experiences. (1968:80)

Donald Winnicott's wife Clare gave Richard Balbernie, the then Principal of the Cotswold Community, a poem which had been written by a 14-year-old boy who later committed suicide. The poem captured how children who were in an unintegrated state experienced their distress and despair. Richard Balbernie then gave the poem to me, as he thought that it was of significance to help my understanding in working with unintegrated children.

He always wanted to explain things.
But no one cared.
So he drew.
Sometimes he would draw and it wasn't anything.
He wanted to carve it in stone or write it in the sky.
And it would be only him and the sky and the
        things inside him that needed saying.
And it was after that he drew the picture.
It was a beautiful picture.
He kept it under his pillow and would let no one see it.
And he would look at it every night and think about it.
And when it was dark, and his eyes were closed, he could still see it.
And it was all of him.
And he loved it.
When he started school he brought it with him.
Not to show anyone, but just to have with him like a friend.
It was funny about school.
He sat in a square, brown desk
Like all the other square brown desks
And he thought it should it be red.
And his room was a square brown room.
Like all the other rooms
And it was tight and close.
And stiff.
He hated to hold the pencil and chalk.
With his arm stiff and his feet flat on the floor
Stiff.
With the teacher watching and watching
The teacher came and spoke to him
She told him to wear a tie like all the other boys.
He said he didn't like them.
And she said it didn't matter!
After that they drew.
And he drew all yellow and it was the way he felt about morning.
And it was beautiful.
The teacher came and smiled at him.
'What's this?' she said. 'Why don't you draw
        something like Ken's drawing?
Isn't that beautiful?'

After that his mother bought him a tie.
And he always drew airplanes and rocket ships like everyone else.
And he threw the old picture away.
And when he lay alone looking at the sky,
It was big and blue and all of everything,
But he wasn't anymore.
He was square inside
And brown,
And his hands were stiff.
And he was like everyone else.
And the things inside him that needed
    saying didn't need it anymore.
It had stopped pushing.
It was crushed.
Stiff.
Like everything else.

Unintegrated children who are overwhelmed by unbearable and unthinkable anxieties may not be able to express their feelings directly in words, but they may communicate symbolically and through their actions. If the child's communication is not noticed and understood, they become fearful of taking the risk again. Winnicott's concept of emotional integration and unintegration highlights that as workers we constantly need to be working at responding rather than reacting to children's difficult, destructive, chaotic and often bewildering behaviour. Their inner world feels very dark, at times emotionally dead, and they view the outside world as being persecutory. If their carers with whom they are beginning to make an attachment cannot respond to their behaviour or try to understand what they are trying to communicate, the danger is that the child will become increasingly lifeless and 'frozen'. This can lead to further breakdown in their environments, at home and at school. The child's sense of hopelessness and helplessness grows and they move further away from reaching a new starting point in their life. The poem so beautifully and tragically illustrates the unbearable emotional turmoil that unintegrated children and young people have to survive if they are to carry on living with reality and all it entails.

To reach the maturational state of emotional integration means to have internalised a sense of living and being as a whole person, starting to connect bits and pieces together. This piecing and holding together first comes from carers who can begin to see the whole child before the child is aware of themselves. The task of working with unintegrated children can be described as piecing or connecting together the fragmented parts of the child.

This brief overview of some aspects of the work of Bowlby and Winnicott shows that there are many similarities and divergences between them. It is recognised they were both absolutely committed intellectually and psychologically to investigating the mother–infant relationship as providing a secure base and sense of individuality in the developing self of the infant. They each examined what needs to be considered when helping a child to manage the reality factors at an internal and external level, and the challenges involved.

Bowlby's work remains in the field of attachment theory and continues to be used today. Winnicott's view of integration and unintegration describes his theory and concept as a precursor to attachment theory. The infant must become integrated if the mother–infant relationship is to develop and the child to continue the maturational process. Bowlby and Winnicott held a deep and sincere admiration for each other's work, while recognising and accepting their differences.

Neuroscience

New pathways towards a clearer understanding of the impact of infantile traumas on the developing child have evolved with progress in neuroscience over the past 20 years. Bessel van der Kolk (2014), one of the world's leading experts on trauma, has referred to Winnicott as the 'founding father of attunement theory', which lies at the heart of attachment.

With advances in neuroscience we are now able to see the brain functioning in ways that illuminate the work of Bowlby and Winnicott. The two men provided an emotional and psychological explanation of something that also has a biological dimension. We are now fortunate to have a new way of seeing and understanding their work. It is a telling point that Dan Siegel, the eminent neuroscientist, says that 'Neural Integration is at the heart of well-being'. All three ways of understanding – Winnicott's integration/unintegration, Bowlby's attachment and recent advances in neuroscience – help us to have greater insight into what is occurring experientially for a child and in how they are making sense of their relationships with others. By seeing the real effects of neglect, trauma and abuse on maturational growth, we can appreciate that our ability and emotional strength to manage reality does not automatically arrive chronologically. Perry (2006) has described the process of neurological development as evolving sequentially and, like Winnicott, shows that a child must work through different stages to develop and mature.

Human growth and development are dependent on the quality of relationships. A baby is born with the brain still growing. The brain continues to grow rapidly through infancy and into childhood, this growth finally concluding in early adulthood. Infants are designed to relate to, recognise and actively respond to their mother's scent, voice and face from birth onwards (Music 2011). The experiences we encounter affect the growth of our brains, and a rich relational environment creates a richness of brain connections. The architecture of the brain comes to represent the architecture of the social environment (Tomlinson, private communication, 2015).

We are constantly seeking to be connecting relationally. Our brains are physically affected by our experiences, then neural connections will fire along pathways established and reinforced by those experiences. This is often referred to in terms of how our brains are 'wired'.

This chapter shows how the experiences of some children will affect the way their brains develop and how nurture will affect the pattern of maturational growth. We can see how a child's natural reactions to the poor experiences of care in early childhood result in repeated behaviours (and reactions to those behaviours) that also affect their developing brains in such a way that they will not achieve the usual maturational growth. We can also become more aware of why the child reacts to this experience in ways their previous experiences have left them wired to do so. The brain develops as a result of use, so those areas most used will develop the most. The predominant emotional and physical experiences will impact on the brain's wiring.

Interactive repair is possible through the plasticity of the brain. Dockar-Drysdale recognised this in 1958, when she explained her preference for the term 'frozen' rather than 'affectionless' because 'affectionless' sounds final, but 'a thaw can follow a frost'. Understanding about cortisol is useful. The chemical cortisol is released in the brain during stress, Its purpose along with adrenaline is to activate preparedness for flight or fight when in danger. In excess, however, due to ongoing stress it begins to have a toxic effect. Emotional stressful factors causing anxiety, depression and insomnia have an effect on hormones in the body and brain, but this does not have to be a permanent state of affairs. Cortisol levels can be influenced by reparative care, and the effects of chronic stress can be ameliorated (Griffin and Ojeda 1996). It is also interesting that Dockar-Drysdale (1958), who was hugely influenced by Winnicott, also used the term 'frozen' long before we knew that excess cortisol actually has a freezing effect on brain growth.

Just as there is hope and hard work in the re-parenting necessary for some young people, so the brain can also change. For example, if distress can be comforted, soothed and contained, then the stress hormones can be lowered. With the regular experiences of attunement, the child's frontal cortex develops a great concentration of receptors to modulate stress. A calm environment is needed for them to work as they should, and this is the responsibility of the primary carers. The child needs good enough primary provision to gradually develop the emotional capacity to regulate their own emotions and accept personal responsibility.

Predictable, responsive parenting and attentive, attuned communication matter. Understanding the communication of a need and responding at the appropriate stage of development leads to a stronger experience of security and self-esteem in the child. The parent needs to be able to regulate the child's anxieties. This will depend on their own ability to regulate their own sense of equilibrium and well-being. It is the sense of security that helps to protect a child from the most damaging effects of trauma. Neuroscience allows us to see the relational happening in the outside world of the child being taken inwards and becoming the internal working model as described by Bowlby. Looking from the internal world outwards, we can see how brain functioning affects the physiology and behaviour of the child. Truly the inner world is made visible in a different way from what we have seen before.

Understanding and applying a well-formulated theoretical concept provides greater clarity about the complexities of the work and can be used to convert our thinking into good therapeutic practice, enabling us to reach the painful inner emotions that have been locked away by the child.

Summary

This chapter has identified how crucial it is that we can reach out to children and young people who, because of their experiences of trauma, hostility, abandonment and breakdown of attachment relationships, are overwhelmed with feelings of panic, rage and unthinkable anxiety. It has placed the work of John Bowlby and Donald Winnicott in context with each other, bringing together a perspective on the individuals and their thinking. Their work has endured the passage of time and provided a legacy of thinking that lives on. With the evolvement of neuroscience as a crucial way of thinking about the impact of traumatic experiences on the developing child, we can see how the three areas of work – attachment, integration and unintegration, and neuroscience – interlink.

Music and colleagues (2011:950) write, 'We might never erase old experiences and brain pathways. There are of course windows of opportunity when big developments take place.' To provide children and young people with new opportunities that can help them gain more from their experiences requires the finding of a new starting point in their life. Bowlby and Winnicott gave us a starting point in developing our thinking about the impact of early experiences on a child's view of reality. Finding the starting point in our work with traumatised children and young people is the beginning of good therapeutic practice. From this we can develop and formulate a positive 'healing process', which understands and responds to children's unmet needs. This provision is the way forwards and vital for the children's recovery. As children begin to feel and believe they exist as people with their own sense of self, they are moving towards 'emotional integration'. From this point they can continue on to the next stage of their journey and maturational development. With support they can begin to think about and manage the realities of the expectations of the outside world, without breaking down.

CHAPTER 3

SYNDROMES OF DEPRIVATION
Finding the Starting Point

Christine Bradley

Introduction

Bowlby and Winnicott have had a significant influence on our understanding of child development. A greater understanding has emerged about the appropriate responses needed to help children through difficult and turbulent periods in their development. It is important that parents and carers can relate to children's emotional anxieties, supporting and helping them through the uncertainties in life. In time, this enables children to become emotionally competent and to manage the challenges of the external world with confidence, energy and enthusiasm. Dockar-Drysdale wrote about the difference between good child care and therapeutic management:

> Good child care is not the same as the preoccupation of the ordinary devoted mother and therapeutic management is again different. However, I do not believe that therapeutic management can be achieved without considerable involvement – something stronger and perhaps more primitive than empathy. (1990:7)

Children and young people whose early years have been subject to abusive and neglectful experiences are often left overwhelmed with feelings of panic, rage, despair and abandonment. These emotions become embedded in their mind and body, as they are unable to communicate to others the emotional pain that influences their view of the outside world and their part in it. The reality they live with becomes too painful and unbearable for them to manage. Feelings of hopelessness and helplessness predominate. They find it impossible to achieve a sense of safety and purpose in their lives. Where behaviour cannot be managed and thought about by others, children are likely to act out destructively to protect themselves. Their actions may be harmful to others as well as to themselves.

Jean Giono, in his book *The Man Who Planted Trees* (1985), describes so accurately the inner world of traumatised children. He writes, 'People who have suffered so long inside that they have forgotten to be free... [T]here are also times in life when a person has to rush off in pursuit of hopefulness' (1985:51). If workers can have a greater insight into the emotional world of traumatised children and young people, it could provide them with a way of working which could help them to develop and strengthen their sense of self, and able to manage the reality of the outside world without breaking down and acting out destructively or self-destructively.

The impact of extreme trauma can result in a split between the child's inner world of emotions and thoughts and their relationship with the outside world. They remain locked inside, unable to relate to the outside world. Without treatment, this can continue throughout life and present as a lack of self-esteem and emotional deadness. Without specialist help, it becomes impossible to achieve a sense of being emotionally alive with a capacity to form healthy relationships. Inevitably, this disrupts their further development. To survive their unbearable feelings, they develop a 'false self', finding it impossible to acquire a good enough sense of a 'real self', with which they can function.

Winnicott wrote:

> The false self is built up on a basis of compliance. It can have a defensive function, which is the protection of the true self. ...only the true self can feel real, but the true self must never be affected by external reality, must never comply. When the false self becomes exploited and treated as real there is a growing sense in the individual of futility and despair. (1965:133)

This chapter will identify how workers can begin to understand and discover the real self, who remains 'trapped' behind the facade which the child or young person presents to the outside world.

Warehousing or therapeutic treatment

The behaviour of children and young people which is difficult to manage in latency and adolescence often relates back to their early childhood traumatic experiences of abuse, abandonment and violence. They may be in need of specialist care, and are often placed in residential homes, foster care, secure unit provision, young offenders' institutions, mental health settings and specialist educational facilities. If they are to recover from the emotional damage caused by their early experiences, they will require an environment which can facilitate the meeting of their emotional needs. These needs may span all aspects of their daily life, or be more specifically related to certain areas. They may need a high level of emotional and physical containment. This is not an easy task for workers, but it is important for it to be understood and achieved.

Decades ago, residential care institutions often held 20–30 children and young people in the same establishment. With so many children and young people in one establishment, and workers who lacked significant training and had little insight and understanding in helping children and young people to feel better about themselves, many children filled with these overwhelming emotions could easily fall into a state of frenzy, often leading them to act out destructively or self-destructively. It is little wonder that workers and carers felt swamped by the disturbance of the children and young people around them. Without support and training, the workers would often 'react' rather than respond therapeutically to the difficult and challenging behaviour. This led to a practice of 'warehousing' under a tightly controlled regime, rather than reaching an understanding about how to meet children's emotional needs.

Without an opportunity to reflect on their practice and explore opportunities for change, it became impossible for workers to respond to children and young people. Inevitably, workers found themselves in a vicious circle and became demoralised. Consequently, there developed an anti-social subculture in these settings, which often led to serious acting out. The underlying difficulties and emotions of rage, persecutory anxiety and panic were repeated and projected onto others in the setting. This resulted in disastrous outcomes for these children and young people. As they did not feel emotionally contained and understood in their placement, the compulsion to repeat their unbearable behaviour continued. Often they would be colluded with as there were no alternatives, and many of the children would end up institutionalised as adults. For example, 85 per cent of young people from the Cotswold Approved School ended up in prison (Miller 1989). Similar patterns can be seen today, when a child is continuously moved due to placement breakdown. Currently there are no longer children's homes with large groups of children and young people in the UK. The model focuses on small numbers of between two and six children, replicating a family environment. There is in addition an increase in the numbers of children and young people who require foster placements or alternative provision.

If workers and carers are to be more in touch with the inner world of children, they need to have the opportunity to reflect on and discuss their own work experiences and how these influence their professional and personal lives. Although the term 'warehousing' is no longer used, there are still many challenges to be faced. The level of emotional turmoil involved in the work is as powerful and often 'primitive' as was observed in the previous era of residential provision. As the need for specialist placements in fostering and residential care continues to be very high, it is important that we understand and meet children's emotional needs. Often providers and commissioners can find themselves under pressure, underestimating the difficulty of the work required, and consequently children and young people can be placed in a setting without access to the caring treatment that they need.

Many of the children have been through a series of traumatic separations, which can result in a feeling of alienation from others. Their difficult behaviour means that placements often break down and the pattern of behaviour is labelled either as an 'attachment disorder' or another diagnostic category. Without a treatment programme being set up to deliver good therapeutic practice to meet children's emotional need, their difficult and anti-social behaviour continues in a compulsive and repetitive manner.

If we are to help children and young people to feel better about themselves, it is important that we are able to practically and emotionally recognise and provide for their needs. This includes supporting and helping them to manage their own anxieties and uncertainties, which break through when they find the outside world too stressful and unbearable. Extensive knowledge and insight are needed by the workers and carers, if the children and young people are to strengthen their sense of relatedness between themselves and others. The workers need to find a way of reaching out to the real self in the children and young people for whom they are responsible. Having access to training and consultation, which present a good overview of therapeutic work and practice, is critical. They need to acquire a deeper understanding about the inner reality of the child and how this shapes their expectations of the external world. Enabling the child to internalise the good experiences from their placement in the residential setting or foster home can influence the child's pattern of thinking with a realisation that a good experience can never be lost. The memory of it can be used at times of stress and pressure, or at later times in their lives when they are having to live through unbearable experiences. The task of good therapeutic practice is to help the child's view of the outside world to become more manageable and bearable.

Therapeutic practice: doing and being Donald Winnicott

Although the syndromes of deprivation based on the work of Winnicott and Dockar-Drysdale were being constructed and placed into working practice 40 years ago at the Cotswold Community and the Mulberry Bush School, they remain as important today. The underlying concepts have provided a pathway to deepening our understanding about the inner world of emotionally fragmented children and young people and should be used to inform current knowledge and practice.

The enormity of the task in hand is described by Williams:

> In addition to their external, often massive deprivation, they are faced with a lack of imagination, vitality, capacity to think and to learn. An internal space is a luxury which they might, for a long time, be unable to afford. (Williams 2002:31)

Clearly there is a need for workers to acquire a deeper understanding of the difficult and challenging behaviour, and what it represents in terms of the earlier experiences of the children and young people with whom they work. These children and young people have missed out on so much emotional understanding and containment and have felt 'invaded' by the negative projections of those caring for them. The task of the worker is to enable the child or young person to move from feelings of hopelessness towards hope.

Donald Winnicott stated that the ability to 'do' is based on the capacity to 'be' (Abram 1996:68). By this he meant the capacity of 'being'. Understanding yourself as an individual underpins the ability to think about yourself and your personal existence. Without the existence of these two elements which are grounded in the real world, the child or young person will construct a 'false self' to enable them to interact both with themselves and with society. The face they present to society is one of charm and compliance; however, their inner world is framed by a primitive anxiety which is so embedded in the emotional pain of early experiences that it must be repressed and cannot be thought about. The capacity to 'be' is to feel secure within oneself, and this should provide children with the foundation from which they can build and emotionally strengthen themselves as individuals.

Most children and young people who are in need of specialist care were not able to achieve a healthy sense of being in their childhood years. For many of them there was a strong environmental failure in their early life experiences. A well-thought-out therapeutic working culture can provide them with the opportunity, through the use of a facilitating environment, which is enough to meet their unmet primary needs and to support their secondary needs. Effective therapeutic work, which enables emotional needs to be communicated, understood and met, can help these children to develop their functioning capacities. This could take them towards achieving a healthy sense of being a person in their own right, from which they can develop and function as an individual. This is the time when 'being and doing' come together, helping children to reach a stage of emotional integration in their day-to-day lives. The beginning of the work is to establish a feeling of safety within which these children can allow themselves to relax and 'be'.

Ten years ago I was visiting a children's home which had evolved successful therapeutic provision. I had been a consultant to them for a lengthy period. Recently I had experienced a serious accident which had left me in hospital and away from work for many months. Although the main purpose of the visit was to meet with the managers and staff team, after our discussion I was asked to spend some time with the children as they wanted to see me. Prior to my accident, I had been working with them on a regular fortnightly basis over several years. Of course, I was delighted to see them, and they were also excited to see me.

There was a teenage girl Annie, who had several foster home breakdowns before she was placed in the home. She had been very difficult, but through the therapeutic work she had received from her workers and carers was now more emotionally contained and could talk about her anxieties and fears. Annie said to me, 'Are you here to help the grown-ups how to understand us today, Christine?' I replied, 'Well, no, I am not able to yet, but I have come over to meet you all and see how you are.' Another child said, 'Ah yes, I know, the grown-ups told us that you had a fall and hurt yourself and had to go to hospital, but you are better now. Does that mean that you will come back?' I replied to her, 'Yes, I will return, but you see when terrible things happen to you and you are very hurt, whether it be physical because of an accident or emotional because of what is happening around you, it is very important to allow yourself to feel looked after and taken care of, then you can feel better about yourself.' Annie replied, 'I used to feel horrible about myself and I wanted everybody else to feel horrible, but since I have been here and the grown-ups are looking after me, I feel better about myself and I do not want to be horrible because I do not need to make people understand me any more. I am pleased that you are not going to die, Christine, and that one day you will be better enough to come back to us.' I said goodbye to them all and returned home to rest. In time, I did make a complete recovery and returned to them. By this time Annie had been moved to a foster home, where she settled in and became very happy. Annie's view of herself because of the therapeutic care and treatment she had received was that she had come to value herself and emotionally develop enough to create a sense of being in the outside world successfully.

Annie's experience illustrates Winnicott's statement that 'early environmental failure can be mended' (Abram 1996:4).

Diagnosis and syndromes

It is difficult to compile a definitive list of the symptoms associated with attachment disorder because of the varying nature and the way it affects different people and relationships. What is clear is that children's behaviour caused from the associations and symptoms of a pathological disorder can create high levels of anxiety and concern in workers and carers. A diagnosis can help them to have a theoretical understanding about this behaviour, providing them with a defence against their own anxieties. However, it cannot present them with the tools to deliver therapeutic practice that can reach out to the 'lost child' who remains hidden behind the defensive wall of their inner world.

As well as viewing behaviour in children and young people that is difficult to manage through a diagnostic category, we need to be working towards acquiring a deeper understanding and insight. We need to understand the meaning of the behaviour – how this relates to traumatic, hostile and abusive experiences during their early childhood and how these experiences have overwhelmed them and arrested their development.

Dockar-Drysdale (1973) used the term 'syndromes of deprivation' in situations where the defences of children, adults or adolescents are as they were originally established during their development as infants and remain unchanged until their needs are met, and they can then begin to grow emotionally.

She described the effect of early trauma on children and young people. Her view was that, without specialist and suitable treatment, the difficulties which severely emotionally deprived children were left with were unlikely to alter. She also outlined the importance for workers and carers to have clarity about when the deprivation and trauma in the child's early life began and when the behaviour became difficult and turbulent in the latency period or adolescence. An understanding of how much of the young person's acting out was a communication about the fears and panic from their previous experiences which had been left inside them was critical (Dockar-Drysdale 1990:67). Along with Donald Winnicott, she developed an outline describing syndromes of deprivation. Their terminology linked current behaviour and emotional difficulties to the traumatic experiences that the child encountered in the early years. This gave the workers a clearer view as to how the child was presenting in their later years when they had not yet developed a 'sense of self', which they could live with and manage the reality factors in their life successfully. The key syndromes are described below:

- The frozen child: a child whose infantile traumas interrupted their development in the first few months of life and this was followed by further abuse and trauma.

- The archipelago child: a child who had some good infantile experiences, but breakdown occurred before they had managed a natural separation from their primary carer.

- The caretaker self: a small child who internalised a good experience but was not able because of traumas and early separation to develop a strong sense of self.

- Fragile integration: similar to the current concept of attachment disorder.

Importantly, the concept of the false self as described by Winnicott (1978:140) can be applied to each of the four syndromes, as a response to the extremes of reality in the lives of both integrated and unintegrated children.

The frozen child

The term 'integration' was originally described by Winnicott (1960) in 'The theory of the parent–infant relationship' as part of the human psyche which develops into a whole being. While the infant can begin its life in a state of primary integration, i.e. beginning to develop a sense of self, unintegration is when the early mother–infant relationship either breaks down or does not begin, and the sense of self is locked away and not allowed to evolve and grow. Winnicott (1960,1965) moved towards providing a theory which saw the child as evolving from the unity of the mother–infant relationship (primary merger) into a secondary relationship where two people relate to one another (the basis of attachment). The three aspects of this unity that facilitate healthy development comprise: holding, leading to integration of sensorimotor elements; autonomy, moving towards personal identity; and object relating, resulting in the establishment of a human relationship (Fonagy 2001).

The traumas of the frozen child relate to the earliest parts of the infant's existence, when their experiences were so full of emotional abandonment, lacking holding, containment and ongoing nurturing by their primary carers, that the centre of their inner world became 'frozen'. If their experiences are compounded by further emotional trauma, their inner world continues to remain 'frozen'. They begin to function only at a superficial level and can very easily break down to act out. This can lead to destructive and self-destructive outcomes in their life.

The concept of the 'frozen child' syndrome developed by Dockar-Drysdale (1958) was used to inform the therapeutic child care and treatment of children at the Mulberry Bush School. Dockar-Drysdale explained that the original trauma related to a time when the primary experiences between a child and primary carer were interrupted. This left the attachment process between the child and primary carer broken off, before the child was ready to make a natural transition to a state of interdependence. As a result, the child built up extreme rather than healthy survival mechanisms. These children were still looking for the symbiotic state they were left in as infants. Consequently, they were floundering and seeking to merge with their environment, consistently disrupting the boundaries around them. Since their survival mechanisms came into being at a very early stage of their life, before they could think, and the primary carer could not 'hold them in mind', they developed their own reality to live with. In their view of the world, what happened yesterday no longer existed. They were not able to learn from their experiences, nor could they accept personal responsibility for their actions. Redl and Wineman (1951) termed such behaviour 'reality blindness', explaining that the child can ignore the inevitable consequences of their behaviour, has no concept of time, and consequently there can be no past to regret and no future to consider. The child lives only in the present.

Dockar-Drysdale (1958:19) wrote that the frozen child presents a curiously contradictory picture.

> He has charm... He is apparently extremely friendly, and seems to make good contacts very quickly. He is frequently generous and kind to younger children, especially one particular child whom he protects against all attacks. In astonishing contrast, he may become suddenly savagely hostile, especially towards a grown-up with whom he has been friendly. He will fly into sudden panic and rages for no apparent reason, in which he snatches and destroys anything in his vicinity... He steals, lies and destroys relentlessly and without the slightest indication of remorse. It is common to hear workers remark: 'It's impossible to believe it is the same child.'

However, if workers can understand and respond to their outbursts of panic, rage and unthinkable anxiety, it is possible for these frozen children to unfreeze and unlock the part of their inner world which felt abandoned, being forced to drag themselves through life without sharing their world with others. To reach such an achievement, workers and carers must be able to 'bear the unbearable' emotions that emerge in the work (Bradley 2010). It is important to consider the following when working with emotionally frozen children and young people:

1. The frozen child cannot manage the intimacy of attachment relationships. Workers need to adapt to meeting their dependency needs in small ways that do not threaten.

2. The child needs to be constantly held in mind by the workers and carers who are responsible for them, because they did not experience this with their primary carer.

3. The child disrupts boundaries and develops their own reality, which for them is safer than living with actual reality.

4. The child has very few areas of functioning in their day-to-day living. These mask panic and rage, which can be acted out destructively and self-destructively under the slightest stress.

The archipelago child

Archipelago children find themselves trapped in their own fragmented world during their maturational development. The term represents a child who has experienced a sense of 'good enough' care and provision from their primary carer, feeling held in mind by them for a period. Unfortunately, this experience has broken down for a variety of reasons before they can become a separate person with their own sense of self. Although they have made their first step towards emotional integration, they have not continued developing through the maturational process. Their sense of self is very raw and fragile, but nevertheless they have the potential inner resources to rebuild their life.

Dockar-Drysdale (1990) described these children as being made up of ego-islets that never fused into a continent, hence the term 'archipelago' (a cluster of islands scattered in the sea). Although archipelago children can function for a period and often enjoy being creative and becoming part of a group setting, their sense of self is fragile and small and they find stress, separation and loss difficult to manage. The underlying reasoning is that early separation happened too early, before they were ready for the transition. This can lead them to panic when they are overwhelmed with anxiety. They cease to function and can return to the emotions from their traumatic experiences when they missed out on the continuity of primary provision. They felt deprived before they were ready to give up their need for dependence with their primary carer. It is important in therapeutic work that carers and workers can identify the child's primary needs and provide appropriate adaptations to meet these needs when required. This can help prevent a return to the panic and rage which became embedded in them earlier in their life. The inner world of the archipelago child has gaps that reflect this deprivation. Their inner world fluctuates between the two aspects (terror and pleasure).

A teenage girl who had been assessed as an archipelago child said, 'Either I want to dance all night and put my pretty dresses on feeling lovely and having some fun, or I want to hide in a dark hole that I will never escape from.' During the time she spent in the home she had been placed in, she could function well, working in an office during the day, successfully being quite methodical and organised, and being helpful in the home. However, she could also break down, ceasing to function and would join in with the anti-social tendency in the group home and the nearby vicinity. This left her carers and workers in the home lost as to how they could help her to feel better about herself. Then they realised that at times they needed to manage her boundaries, without making her feel as if they were attacking her. This was followed by a realisation that the level of her self-esteem was so low that the slightest stress could prevent her from functioning. She was demonstrating her own underlying sense of worthlessness and hopelessness.

An archipelago child can move from being gentle, concerned about others and dependent on their workers and carers, to being aggressive and hostile to others at quite a primitive level. However, it is important to remember that the child did reach the starting point of integration. The continuity in development was interrupted, and there was no transition to a clear sense of personal identity. A well-thought-through treatment programme could help such a child progress to achieving emotional integration. The main objective is to anticipate and help bridge the gaps between one island of functioning and another, so that the child does not fall into a sea of chaos.

Key points to remember when working with the archipelago child or young person:

1. The child's areas of functioning need supporting, while their areas of non-functioning are locked into an early infantile state of loss that needs to be provided for and adapted to.

2. When the child falls into their emotional gaps and ceases to function, their depression and despair are very deep. They can become self-destructive and self-harming, and their self-esteem disintegrates.

3. The child expects failure when under stress and needs a great deal of support to survive the unbearable sense of loss and fears of abandonment.

4. When the child is functioning, they need continuing support from their carers and workers to keep them going through difficult times.

The caretaker self

This syndrome represents the child who in their early years experienced significant good experiences from a carer – if not the mother, perhaps a foster carer, a grandmother, an aunt – or a period in a specialist residential setting. The important thing is that the child felt emotionally contained and held in mind by their carer. Unfortunately, their good primary experiences were interrupted by trauma and separation before the small child was ready to manage the transition towards interdependence. This means that they had made an attachment relationship with their primary carer and had internalised good primary experiences with them, but experienced a sense of loss before they were ready to let go of their identification with their carer. The loss of their carer traumatised them to the extent that they are unable to attach to another individual. Their early loss impedes their developmental growth and transition into the next stage in their life.

Although emotionally fragile, they become their own 'caretaker' acting as a gatekeeper to their sense of self, but find it difficult to relate to other people and manage the presentation of reality.

However, because their sense of loss and abandonment took place after a satisfactory experience of absolute dependency and some continuity of care, they are more able to think about their unbearable feelings. Although they become prone to wild temper tantrums because of a deep sense of sadness, they can be reached emotionally by others through communication, which can prevent the acting out associated with feelings of panic and rage.

> Charlie was a 14-year-old boy who had been assessed as a 'caretaker child'. He returned home from school early when I was having my first meeting with the staff team at the home he was living in. He was angry that I had taken his carers away from providing him with some food and drink on his return. He disrupted the meeting and began to climb the curtains. I apologised to him and explained that I was not aware that he would be so upset. He said to me, 'Well, they always give me special food and drink when I come home, and I cannot do it myself. I do not like it when they are not there.' I said to him, 'Is it that you feel you have been forgotten about? He replied, 'Yes, I do.' I suggested that the grown-ups in the home teach Charlie how to cook and make drinks for himself, so that he would be able to make himself a special cup and plate that would be only his. They did adapt to his needs and Charlie felt that he really did matter to his carers. It also meant that Charlie's little self who still needed looking after was being recognised by the carers. Eventually, he left the home and became a successful chef.

It is important that carers and workers can recognise the little self which has become locked inside the caretaker and allow the child or young person to gradually hand the 'caretaker' over to them. It may be important that the child can continue some aspects of their own caretaking. This may help with their self-esteem, while at the same time allowing the child to have important experiences of being taken care of. This helps the little self to feel looked after again, and to develop and mature. Caretaker selves can find verbal communication difficult, but they do have the capacity to communicate symbolically and can be creative in their actions and sense of 'doing'.

Key points to remember when working with the caretaker child:

1. The child needs support to hand the caretaker over to the worker or carer. This should be done through a process of negotiation that allows the 'caretaker self' to feel in control, to be the little self who became stuck in their early years. This could happen in a symbolic way, for example through the use of a third object such as a toy or a piece of cloth.

2. The child needs support for their confidence, which can be fragile at times, particularly when they are dealing with separation and loss in their day-to-day living. These children find transitions difficult to manage.

3. All good experiences need to have a beginning, a middle and an end to make them into a complete experience. This continuity is missing from the caretaker child's early life.

4. The child needs a structured primary experience to fill in their missing emotional gaps when their needs were not able to be met.

5. The emotional outbursts of a caretaker child resonate more with their experiences as a child of two to four years when they had 'temper tantrums' around their feelings of anger and sadness. In general, this can be understood and talked about, because they can think about their actions. It is different from panic and rage, which belong to an earlier experience in their life and which cannot be worked through and thought about.

Fragile integration

The syndrome fragile integration is comparable to insecure attachment disorder. It signifies a situation where even though the infant and small child did make a relationship with a primary carer, the attachment did not form a secure enough base to enable a satisfactory resolution between the needs of their inner world and the demands of the external world. This leaves the fragile integrated child with difficult challenges and a sense of unresolved trauma and loss. Their sense of self can be vulnerable, and this emotional fragility and lack of organisation means that they are unable to resolve issues in their day-to-day lives.

A good and well-organised therapeutic treatment programme implemented by carers and workers can help the child to reintegrate, come back together as a person and carry on with their passage to full emotional integration. They need to return to an attachment relationship with the adult to complete the process of integration.

Key points to remember when working with the fragile integrated child:

1. The child disintegrates when overwhelmed with stress. At a fragile stage of emotional integration, the child or young person is not yet strong enough to feel able to hold onto anxiety and stress without strong support from their carer.

2. The child may push boundaries in an anti-authority though non-panicky way. Workers need to explain to them the difficulties that they are facing.

3. A fragile integrated child did receive enough good early experiences at both a primary and secondary level. They can function, although at times they can become very fragile and need continuous support.

4. The child has a developing sense of self, not yet strong enough to manage stressful factors in their life. Without support from their carers they can remain emotionally stuck in their maturational development.

Conclusion

Before workers can begin to discuss and plan an emotional need assessment and treatment programme, they need to have acquired a clear understanding about the syndromes of deprivation within which the child is situated. This chapter has presented an outline of the internal world of children and young people, examining the impact of early traumatic and abusive experiences on their lives. The aim has been to help workers respond to their behaviour with a clearer understanding of how children's challenging behaviour can represent difficult and painful emotional experiences that emerge from the trauma and pain they have internalised because of early experiences of abuse and neglect.

CHAPTER 4

ASSESSING THE NEEDS OF TRAUMATISED CHILDREN

Christine Bradley

Introduction

In the previous chapters, we have focused on the impact of abusive and traumatic experiences on children in their early life, discussing how it can affect and influence their view of reality later in their lives. It is recognised that such circumstances can leave young children consumed with emotions of panic and rage, making it impossible for them to manage the demands of reality. Their lack of emotional regulation and their overwhelming fear drive them to 'act out' or externalise their difficult emotions through their behaviour. This behaviour disrupts the world around them, and can prevent other children from functioning. To help them to feel better about themselves and more able to manage the external world without breaking down, we need to have a clear view about the specific aspects of their emotional development which remain stuck and trapped at an infantile and early childhood stage. Trowell wrote:

> The incidence of depression in children has increased markedly over the last few years. Children do not just get better of their own accord. They go on to lead limited lives, underachieving at school, at risk of consuming drugs and alcohol, and finding themselves increasingly in social isolation, suffering repeated depressive episodes. If these children have symptoms of anxiety, their prognosis is all the more worrying. (2011:34)

Bowlby's (1988) concept of the secure base remains a crucial factor in child development. He saw the formation of a secure protective attachment evolving from a secure relational base with a primary carer. Moving on from the psychodynamic tradition, he considered relationships in the external world to be as significant as those in the internal world. Winnicott (1958) viewed the 'symbiotic merger' between mother and baby as a stage of 'absolute dependence', a critical experience if the infant is to move towards a state of interdependence reliant on others for support, while at the same time developing a strong and growing sense of self. Such a child evolves to become an individual, emotionally integrated and self-regulated in managing their painful emotions. This makes it possible for them to share the world with others and keep to the rules.

Through many years of reflective practice and thought, I have discussed the most positive way forward in helping traumatised children to feel emotionally stronger and more positive about their sense of self and their future life. I have come to the realisation that if their emotional needs can be assessed, identified and acknowledged, it will help workers to gain some insight into and understanding of the fragmentation that exists in the child's internal world. It can also help them to respond effectively to difficult and destructive behaviour, which prevents the child from functioning in the external world. Most importantly, it can help the worker to make links between the child's current behaviour and experiences of trauma and abuse in early childhood. It is at this point that therapeutic care and treatment can begin.

How do we find the starting point if we are to develop a sound therapeutic practice from which we can provide children with significant and meaningful relationships? In posing this question, we are aiming for the child to take in and internalise positive experiences from the time spent in their placement with new and different carers. This will enable them to move on to the next stage of their life with an emotional strength. It will help them to manage the challenges of the external world with a belief in themselves as an individual.

> Our psychoanalytic starting point is the idea that there is an internal dimension of children's experience. In the inner world of unconscious phantasy to which we have access in dreaming and through the part of our personalities which responds to symbolic or cultural experiences, the primary focus is on our intimate emotional experiences. (Rustin and Rustin 1966:165)

The view of Rustin and Rustin is that children cannot always use words to express deeply held feelings when their emotions have become embedded in their internal world. Many of the children who need specialist care, whose experiences have been so traumatic and abusive that they are haunted by nightmares, remain stuck in a negative cycle that has no exit. The use of emotional need assessment and therapeutic treatment programmes can provide the way forward for these children.

The emotional need assessment and treatment plan

In 1970, Dockar-Drysdale was working as a therapeutic adviser to the Mulberry Bush School and the Cotswold Community to help them understand the symptomatic behaviour in an unintegrated child (Dockar-Drysdale 1990:188). Her need assessment identified the level of privation and deprivation and the impact this had on the developing self. It also became the base for the formulation of a treatment programme, which could identify the quality of support and provision needed if children were to recover from their early traumatic and abusive experiences. The type of provision they needed depended on the level of emotional integration or unintegration they had reached. The main purpose of both the need assessment and treatment plan was to help the child reach a level of personal identity and emotional integration – a sense of self they could live with.

To make the plan work successfully, it is important to realise that the primary task of the need assessment currently being used is not to 'diagnose' the child; nor is it to label the child as having a specific mental health disorder or illness. It is to identify the fragmented aspects in their emotional life and how those caring for them can meet their unmet needs. In the early days of therapeutic practice, the outcomes for those children who had an assessment and treatment programme were more successful than for those who were placed in a more institutionalised setting. A follow-up study of the Cotswold Community in 1982, many years after it made the transition from an approved school to a therapeutic community using emotional need assessment programmes, showed significant results. Young people returning to prison or continuing to need other specialist care had dropped from 85 per cent to 5 per cent (Miller 1986), such was the impact of assessing the emotional needs of the young people and working towards meeting and providing for their needs.

Over the past 15 years, I have continued to work with the need assessment programme and have developed it in a variety of settings with an ongoing success rate. Although the professional climate and culture have changed considerably, what should not change is the quality of practice that results in children feeling better about themselves, with a stronger sense of self that they are more comfortable with when facing the demands of external reality.

> The young person who is in 'bits', suffering from a distortion of many aspects of their personality, some which need to split off in the unconscious, is certainly not functioning as a whole person. The assessment programme points to those crucial aspects of the personality which determine how far a young person is integrated, and can cope with life and make relationships. (Hardwick and Woodhead 1992:117)

The assessment programme continues to provide a route for practice that can take an unintegrated child through to emotional integration. This process enables them to develop a sense of stronger emotional stability, feeling more whole as a person and able to form attachment relationships with their carers. The use of this need assessment programme can lead to a more stable child who is better able to regulate their emotions, manage feelings related to their past experiences and face the challenges ahead for them (Bradley 2010).

The assessment and treatment plan aims to identify the emotional needs of a child who has been exposed to repeated trauma in their early years. This process can also help workers to develop their insight and understanding about their need for specific practice skills. It influences the quality of the meaningful attachment relationships they can make with children. The development of an attachment relationship within which new and positive experiences are provided for the child can create links between the fragmented parts of the child's development, which can then grow. The child can begin to develop a sense of self based on good experiences. Consequently, as they develop a sense of trust with their worker, they become more able to communicate and reflect on their difficult feelings. Through a sense of safety and attachment, the capacity to regulate emotions begins to develop. The child becomes less hypervigilant and has more space for calm, settled and satisfying feelings. As their good feelings about themselves strengthen, the emotions of panic and rage begin to diminish. With appropriate help and support, in time they begin to function in their day-to-day living without breaking down. If we can help a child to reach a realisation that the emotions in their internal world are not there to be attacked by the outside world, and that the two worlds can learn to live alongside each other, it is a huge achievement for them. Just as in infancy, it is only with the necessary provision from a carer within a holding environment that this can occur.

The point we want to reach with children in successful therapeutic practice is described in the book *Dibs in Search of Self* (Axline 1990:2).

> Slowly, tentatively, he discovered that the security of his world was not wholly outside himself, but that the stabilising centre he searched for with such intensity was deep down inside that self.

Need assessments and treatment programmes can provide the starting point for developing the required skills of therapeutic practice. They define a route and pathway through which workers can take children from unintegration to integration. In beginning to establish strong attachment relationships, the child begins to feel more whole and individual as a person.

Using the emotional need assessment programme

The two primary questions Dockar-Drysdale asked when assessing whether a child was unintegrated or integrated were as follows:

- *Does the child panic?* Panic is defined as a state of unthinkable anxiety.

- *Does the child disrupt?* This question asks whether the child who feels that they cannot exist on their own – and in order to survive – has the need to disrupt others by breaking up something between two or more people.

If the answer to both these questions is yes, the hypothesis is that the child is unintegrated. This will be examined in further detail during the assessment. Further assessment questions identify the level of unintegration.

Since 1970, much thought has been given to the need assessment to ensure it continues to be useful for professionals. Hardwick and Woodhead (1992) identified 20 dimensions of a child's personality that should be addressed if we are to intervene successfully. In developing my own assessment programme, I have introduced seven dimensions. These focus on the child's day-to-day living experiences, identifying how they can or cannot manage them. The current assessment framework is designed to help workers to identify the children's emotional needs, which require appropriate support and provision after an assessment has been completed.

The seven dimensions of a child's day-to-day living experiences we focus on are:

1. boundaries, merging and functioning

2. containing emotion, anxiety, anger and stress

3. self-destruction and self-preservation

4. communication

5. learning from experience

6. play

7. fragile integration.

Thinking about children's emotional needs while completing the assessment enables workers to recognise the trigger points and challenging behaviour as these build up, and to intervene effectively. It also helps them to understand the content of children's emotional needs. This requires the worker to provide well-thought-through and structured positive experiences of nurture and care over time. Alternatively, when children's emotional needs require considerable support from workers, the assessment addresses them from a deeper understanding of the link between emotions and different aspects of their day-to-day living. It also identifies the provision necessary to help the child move towards a sense of hopefulness and competence when they are managing the challenges of the outside world.

How does the programme work?

A need assessment can be an effective tool to clarify problems and strengths and identify appropriate interventions for children's emotional difficulties. It is a process for identifying and addressing their emotional needs when there are gaps in understanding of their functioning and non-functioning in day-to-day living.

Each category of the programme addresses different dimensions of the child's character and focuses on the four syndromes of deprivation – frozen, archipelago, caretaker and fragile integration – as outlined in the previous chapter. It gives us more information about how the child's infantile experiences and early childhood traumas disrupted their maturational process, leaving them in the unintegrated stage of emotional development.

The seven dimensions in detail

1 Boundaries, merging and functioning

In this section, we examine how the child can hold on to boundaries with a sense of personal responsibility. The three key terms used within the tables that follow are defined below.

Boundaries

Boundaries are defined as a line marking the limits of a physical, symbolic or emotional area. A boundary divides territory, creating borders between each area of living and being. Generally, these boundaries must be managed effectively to maintain healthy functioning. Unintegrated children find it difficult to hold on to boundaries. If their primary needs remain unmet, their emotions become overwhelming and dysregulated. This can result in them losing a sense of their own and others' boundaries.

Merging

Merging occurs when all sense of boundaries between self and others is either non-existent or temporarily lost, resulting in a sense of over-identification between two people and an undifferentiated self through a 'primary' merger. When two or more children merge, any sense of self and, separation is lost. Unintegrated children are very vulnerable to merging and, when they do, it can create a powerful and destructive force that will resist any attempt to break up and separate the individuals. They are unable to take responsibility for their individual actions. This can lead to dangerous acting out that has no regard for the safety of self or others.

Functioning

The functioning child can perform a task, meeting the expectations of others without breaking down, managing the challenges it presents to them. To function means to keep on going in the face of the challenge, so the task becomes a complete experience with a beginning, a middle and an end. These complete experiences help establish the building block from which maturational development grows. Functioning can break down when the stress factors become too great to manage and work through. Therefore, support from another can help maintain positive functioning.

Children who have been exposed to physical and emotional abandonment in their early years find holding on to boundaries and keeping to the rules difficult to manage, due to a lack of emotional containment during their formative years. This leaves them with few inner controls and a lack of personal boundaries. It is important that workers can manage the external boundaries, which children must stay within and hold on to. This needs to be worked through internally, rather than the child conforming through external systems of rewards and sanctions.

The following tables (4.1–4.7) present a need assessment model that, in posing key questions, enables the worker to navigate the complex interrelationship between characteristics and categories to reach the child's real self.

Table 4.1: Boundaries, merging and functioning

Key question	Defining characteristics	Category
Does the child merge and disrupt the functioning of others?	A frozen child was traumatised at a very early stage of infantile development, leaving them feeling completely abandoned by their primary carer, emotionally and physically. They continue to constantly seek the 'symbiotic' state that they missed during their early life. They seek to merge with others and their environment, consistently disrupting the boundaries around them. The disruptive activity of a frozen child can be acted out through the panic and rage they are consumed with, because they did not feel held in the mind of their primary carer. They find it extremely difficult to relate to the realities of the external world, can break down and act out destructively. As well as harming others, they are also likely to harm themselves, and have little sense of self-preservation. If a child tends to merge and disrupt, this is a frozen child who will benefit by having one or two people especially focused on providing a close attuned relationship.	**Frozen child** The child requires the provision of good primary experiences, which are consistent, in a well-structured and thought-out setting. The carer or worker needs to become attuned with the child, holding them in their mind.
Does the child have several areas of functioning? Is help needed when functioning breaks down or can the child manage stress and transitions?	The archipelago child has areas of their day-to-day living in which they can function, sharing the world with others and keeping to rules. Because their sense of self can be emotionally raw and quite fragile at times of stress, they can begin to fall apart. They may regress back to their inner world to feelings of hopelessness and helplessness, and to the times in their life when their emotional needs were unmet. They require significant help and emotional support when their functioning breaks down; otherwise they may become overwhelmed with despair, which could place them in danger of self-harming. An archipelago child can be described as having 'islands of ego in a sea of chaos'. A key task is to support the child in making the bridge between one island of functioning and another without falling into the chaos.	**Archipelago child** The child requires considerable emotional support when their functioning breaks down. At this stage, workers and carers need to adapt to their primary needs, helping them to feel emotionally contained during these difficult periods.

cont.

Key question	Defining characteristics	Category
When under stress does the child merge and disrupt the functioning of others?	A caretaker child can be disruptive as they tend to feel they are a caretaker in charge of themselves and others. Although a caretaker child did have some good experiences as a small child, which they internalised, they were nevertheless traumatised and separated from the attachment relationship with their primary carer before they had made a natural transition to the next stage of their emotional development. Under stress they may return to being the small child who is still fragile and needs looking after and taking care of. However, there is a small measure of emotional integration in them and they are not so overwhelmed by feelings of panic and rage, which can often be acted out either destructively and self-destructively. Instead, they act out powerful and angry temper tantrums, which with support and provision from their carer can be worked through and thought about. With appropriate support and concern, a caretaker child can learn from their experiences. It is important for workers to realise that when a caretaker child becomes a small child again, they can allow themselves to be looked after and come to depend on others using the provision which is offered to them. A caretaker child has learned to 'look after' and make self-provision for their fragile self. This has been a necessary survival mechanism. It is important to let the child hand over aspects of their care, when they feel safe and ready to do that.	**Caretaker child** The worker or carer needs to allow the child to hand the caretaker over to them symbolically. The child can regress back to the little self, which can be provided for and feel able to emotionally grow and evolve.

2 Containing emotion, anxiety, anger and stress

A child who cannot think about their emotions of anxiety, anger and stress will become more intense, dysregulated and negative about themselves and others. Unintegrated children cannot think about their actions. They need workers who are aware of their difficulties and who can contain their anxiety and stress, as otherwise, they are in danger of acting out destructively and self-destructively.

Table 4.2: Containing emotion, anxiety, anger and stress

Key question	Defining characteristics	Category
Can they contain emotions, or do they act out violently?	With the emotionally frozen child, the acceptance of external reality is often too unbearable. They did not experience a sense of being held in the mind of the primary carer in their formative years. As a survival mechanism, they develop their own reality, which does not match the reality of the outside world and all it entails. Challenge and confrontation from others, or anything that frustrates their immediate gratification, fills them with panic. This results in acting out, sometimes violently. A frozen child finds it very difficult if not impossible to accept personal responsibility for their behaviour and to learn from their experiences. Usually they feel no remorse or concern for others. Their feelings of despair, inner emptiness and emotional abandonment are so powerful that they are unable to deal with them on their own.	**Frozen child** Workers and carers need to make adaptations to their primary needs, providing certain experiences for them that they become dependent on.
Do they act out violently when under stress?	An archipelago child can function for periods in their day-to-day living. However, there are gaps and spaces in their inner world. They find stress factors in their life difficult to deal with. When they become emotionally fragile, they are in danger of acting out violently. When they become overwhelmed with feelings of despair, they can become self-destructive. Their despair often relates to their early years, when they felt emotionally abandoned by their primary carer.	**Archipelago child** Workers and carers need to have a realisation about their level of functioning being minimal at times. It's important to recognise how their despair can overwhelm them, and to continue to provide emotional support.

cont.

Key question	Defining characteristics	Category
Do they react violently under pressure or perceived threat?	With a caretaker child, their temper tantrums can at times reflect the primitive behaviour of a two-year-old even though they may be much older. Because they felt abandoned by their primary carers before they were ready to separate, their emotions remain locked into that stage of development. Their angry and sometimes violent behaviour often represents a very small child who lives mostly in their inner world. They try to remain in control of their behaviour, but are not always able to. It is important to remember that caretaker selves do have emotional strength to work through the difficult periods and emotions that emerge in their day-to-day living, but require a great deal of support.	**Caretaker child** Workers and carers need to be aware of the child's temper tantrums and what they represent from their past experiences. The child requires help to communicate what is happening to their emotions. Workers and carers must allow them to think through their behaviour.

3 Self-destruction and self-preservation

If a child has no sense of self-esteem they are often not able to take care of themselves. Their level of despair is so great they become overwhelmed by a sense of self-reprisal for their behaviour. They may then react by turning on themselves after acting out their anger, panic and rage with others. Workers need to develop a plan that helps them to feel emotionally contained and nurtured through their difficult periods of hopelessness and helplessness.

Table 4.3: Self-destruction and self-preservation

Key question	Defining characteristics	Category
Do they have very low self-esteem and cannot take care of themselves?	A frozen child has little or no self-esteem. Their sense of self has never broken through their emotionally frozen areas. They are careless and unable to take care of themselves. Any attempt from the adult to take care of them can result in hostile and aggressive responses. These responses have built up as a way of surviving their unbearable feelings and they do not have healthy defence mechanisms. The difficulty is that they can easily break down; their violence and rage will erupt and in these states they will show no sense of concern or empathy. At that time, they are not able to accept personal responsibility for their actions, nor can they learn from their experiences.	**Frozen child** The child needs to feel emotionally contained by their worker. They cannot manage their own painful feelings.
Under stress, can they take care of themselves, or do they show a range of symptoms from self-mutilation to suicidal gestures?	The archipelago child did have some good experiences in their early life, but these were disrupted too early for them. Experiences of trauma, hostility and abuse have resulted in areas of their inner world becoming self-destructive. Small stress factors in their day-to-day living experiences can prevent them from functioning. They may only be able to function well with others for short periods. If their carers or workers react to them, it can result in them acting out destructively or self-destructively. Feelings of despair and depression take over, preventing them from functioning.	**Archipelago child** Workers need to be aware when the child is ceasing to function, and to respond to them accordingly to help prevent a breakdown.
Can they protect themselves? Is their self-preservation haphazard?	The caretaker child experienced a continuity of good care in early life. Unfortunately, the care they received finished too early for them to make a natural transition to the next stage of their development. Although there is a small ego in their inner world, it remains hidden and deprived. They have difficulty holding on to and internalising good experiences. To survive their reality, they have become their own caretaker. Because they became a caretaker to themselves, they are not able to relate to an adult or carer with meaning or through an attachment. To protect themselves they take care of others rather than allow adults or carers to take care of them.	**Caretaker child** If workers and carers can become the caretaker who takes care of the child's little self, it will help the little self to evolve.

cont.

4 Communication

All children can communicate, but we must realise that some, because they are emotionally overwhelmed by the pain and anxiety of their early experiences, simply do not have the words to say how they feel. Such children can often break down, leading to acting out of unbearable feelings. Their development may have been so disrupted, especially if it was pre-verbal, that the ability to communicate has not developed. For therapeutic work to be successful, we need to assess and identify how the capacity to communicate about feelings can prevent acting out.

Table 4.4: Communication

Key question	Defining characteristics	Category
Can the child talk meaningfully in a one-to-one situation, or do they just chatter without meaning?	With a child who is emotionally frozen, their inner world is so full of panic, despair and rage they cannot find the words to express their emotions. Although they will chatter, their words will not explain any of their behaviour and why they need to act out their emotions destructively. Although a baby is unable to speak, it is only when they feel held in the mind of their primary carer that they can feel emotionally contained enough to express themselves.	**Frozen child** Be aware that the difficult and at times unbearable behaviour of frozen children can be an expression of emotions that they cannot verbally communicate about. Workers need to consistently respond to their behaviour.
Is there the potential for some communication, but they back off when anxious or stressed?	Archipelago children find it very difficult to communicate verbally. It is more likely they will communicate symbolically and non-verbally. Their acting out can be seen as an attempt to communicate their despair. This has been referred to by James Anglin (2003) as pain-based behaviour. It can be very difficult for workers to respond to them when they cannot use words to communicate about their anxieties. They can easily fall into the 'dark holes' of their inner world of emotions, about which they cannot communicate.	**Archipelago child** They need as many opportunities for communication in their day-to-day living as possible. A clear understanding of verbal and non-verbal communication is needed.

| Does the child communicate in a way that is not easily understood and often symbolic? | Caretaker children often communicate at a symbolic level. As with a small child, they may communicate through the symbolic language of play.

It is important that workers realise the 'caretaker self' looks after their own 'little self' who remains locked inside, to protect themselves from the outside world.

Using symbolic communication, playing and creativity, in time they can turn their symbols into verbal communication. | **Caretaker child**

It is important to reach and maintain a level of symbolic communication between workers/carers and the child. |

5 Learning from experience

Learning from experience means the child can take in cognitively and emotionally what is happening in the world around them, and think about the consequences of their actions. Unintegrated children find learning from experience difficult. Their sense of self and self-belief is so fragile that feelings of hopelessness and helplessness overpower their desire to learn. Without a great amount of support and provision from their carers they can find themselves constantly repeating their bad experiences. This leaves little space for their good experiences to be learned from and internalised by them. Learning from experiences is on two levels – emotional and cognitive. A healthily developing child begins to recognise the consequences of their own actions. This leads to a desire to repair the damage they cause emotionally and physically to others.

Table 4.5: Learning from experience

Key question	Defining characteristics	Category
Can the child learn from their personal, social and school experiences, including mistakes?	A frozen child does not and cannot learn at school and can become school phobic, often excluded and very behind for their age. It is difficult for teachers to help them to learn, because their experience of learning and being part of a group becomes unbearable for them. They can often disrupt the classroom and refuse to learn. Because they cannot internalise good experiences, their mentalisation process can be very limited. The only mirror image for a frozen child is one of absence, hostility and abuse.	**Frozen child** They need a great deal of one-to-one help to learn from their experiences, and for teaching purposes, before they feel emotionally strong enough to become part of a group and share the world with others.
Does the child have the potential to learn cognitively and emotionally, through communication, but lose it under stress?	The archipelago child does have the capacity to learn, but under stress they expect to fail. Because they blame themselves for difficulties in their life, their fear of failure is easily activated. They are in danger of acting out their sense of despair, becoming destructive to themselves and to others, and their capacity to function diminishes.	**Archipelago child** They need constant support from their carers and teachers. Their fear of failure needs to be supported therapeutically so that they can continue with their challenges.
Does the child find learning at school a difficult experience?	With a caretaker self the reality of having to learn about a difficult and painful experience personally, socially or educationally can be very threatening to their small ego. The caretaker can take over their life, leaving the frightened little self trapped inside them. With help and support from their carers who can take care of their little self, they start to learn through their relationship. They can learn generally and are more able to grow intellectually and emotionally over time.	**Caretaker child** Workers and carers need to help the little self to find their own way of learning intellectually and emotionally through creative and symbolic support.

6 Play

Children and young people who did not experience the feeling of being held in the mind of their primary carer during the first year of life lack the capacity for symbolic play. They find it difficult to enjoy playing on their own, or with adults and children (McMahon 1992). It can also result in difficulty communicating their emotions verbally or symbolically.

Unintegrated children are not yet ready to play and share with other children. They did not experience a safe place for playing when they were infants, and do not feel safe enough in themselves to be able to play on their own with pleasure. They need a high level of feeling held in the mind of their carer in their home, who will play with them at a primary level. As they move towards emotional integration in their day-to-day living, they will be able to find a safe space to play in and start to engage in group play without being disruptive.

Table 4.6: Play

Key question	Defining characteristics	Category
Has the child ever learned how to play?	A frozen child did not have the opportunity to play with their primary carer. The carer's lack of attunement and mirroring did not provide the necessary other to play with. The same lack of attunement would have caused their feelings to be dysregulated. Consequently, because they are so overwhelmed with anxiety, it is not possible for them to play on their own with pleasure. It is more likely that they will disrupt play experiences both for themselves and other children in group settings.	**Frozen child** The child requires opportunities for appropriate primary provision through play experiences.
Is the child's play easily distracted and sometimes destructive?	Because of the functioning and non-functioning areas in the archipelago child, they fluctuate between creative and destructive feelings. It can result in them breaking down and acting out when they fall into their non-functioning areas. Although they can play at times with others, they can find it difficult to make good use of play opportunities. Unstructured play might be quite anxiety provoking. Due to difficulties with transitions, they might find it difficult to complete a play experience.	**Archipelago child** The child requires individual play opportunities with workers and carers and to be supported in creating transitional play.

cont.

Key question	Defining characteristics	Category
Can the child play, but at an infantile level?	A caretaker child can use their play experiences to communicate at a symbolic level, communicating about their own traumatic experiences. They can use their play materials to demonstrate their own sense of self. They can express their own awareness about how they experience the outside world, either as an attacking and hostile environment or a place to be a part of in which they feel comfortable.	**Caretaker child** They require play material for symbolic play, which they can communicate through, and their worker or carer can consider the meaning of this.

7 Fragile integration

A fragile integrated child is one who is beginning to come together as a person. The child has reached a stage in development where they have a sense of self, although at times of stress they can disintegrate and fall apart for a short while. Because they have now begun to internalise a secure base for their emotional development, they do come together again and, with support, learn from their painful experiences. At this stage, they are ready to make attachment relationships with their workers, although they still find stress factors difficult to manage and need considerable emotional support.

The assumption that underlies the concept of fragile integration is that the links between the fragmented aspects of the child's inner world are beginning to form. Consequently, the key terms that have been used to date, namely the frozen, archipelago and caretaker child, have been superseded by emotional integration. At times of stress, the child may revert to one of these earlier states, but has the capacity to work through these difficult periods, learning from experience.

A number of key questions are asked that enable the carer to identify the emotional needs of the child and how the impact of their traumatic experiences affects their day-to-day living.

Table 4.7: Fragile integration

Key question	Defining characteristics
Can the child hold on to boundaries, but push them in an anti-authority way, especially under stress?	A fragile integrated child is beginning to develop a sense of self, and can hold on to boundaries when not under stress and anxiety. However, they are not yet strong enough to be able to manage stress without at times breaking down and acting out. They still need considerable emotional support from their workers if they are to continue strengthening their level of emotional integration, with a developing sense of inner confidence about who they are.
Do they disintegrate when very anxious and are unable to talk about stress?	At a fragile state of integration, the child is not yet strong enough to have the emotional resources to hold on to persistent anxiety and stress, which can occur within different experiences, such as the family, their placement, group experiences and education. They also find it difficult to continually accept personal responsibility for their behaviour. The treatment plan will help them to be more able to express their stressful periods and the anxiety they create. Slowly their emotional integration will begin to grow.
Under stress, do they lack self-esteem and self-care, and can they become self-destructive?	Although a fragile integrated child is beginning to come together as a person and make attachment relationships, they can at times revert to the point of the earlier breakdown. It is important that their workers can recognise what could throw them into this situation, and provide them with the support to work through difficult and at times unbearable emotions. Although they have developed a sense of self, and can function in their day-to-day living, they are emotionally fragile.
Is communication more at a symbolic level, with little investment in verbal communication? Do they find it difficult to face reality and when out of communication break down into anti-social behaviour?	These children have reached a sense of self in their inner world. However, when reality becomes too stressful for them, they become emotionally raw and can break down into anti-social behaviour and delinquent acting out. Although they can verbally communicate, they may revert to communicating at a symbolic or non-verbal level. Workers need to remain aware that if communication should fail, they may regress to 'acting out'.

cont.

Key question	Defining characteristics
Does the child have a general commitment to school and the experiences that are offered to them?	The child has achieved a sense of self, and is on the edge of emotional integration, i.e. coming together as a person. Progress can be poor and they sometimes repeat mistakes in their behaviour and levels of functioning. If they have opportunities to talk about their fears and anxieties, with their workers alongside them emotionally, they can begin to learn and take a strong interest in what they are doing.
Does the child engage in solitary or co-operative play?	A fragile integrated child can play on their own with pleasure when they are functioning, and can share their play experiences with others. Under stress, however, they can break down and disrupt the play of others. Unlike an unintegrated child, they have the capacity to think through their actions afterwards. They have the potential to repair disruptive behaviours through expressions of concern, guilt and reparation, demonstrating their connection with reality.

Once the appropriate questions have been answered and recorded, the information can be used to develop the therapeutic treatment programme. This will give workers a plan from which the child's emotional needs can be worked through, provided for, and met.

Guidance in using the need assessment

- The assessment meeting should involve all workers who are or have been engaged in the child's life over the past 12 months.

- The chair of the meeting and everyone involved should have as much information as possible about the first few years of the child's life, their relationship with their primary carer and any significant events.

- Do not ask all the questions on the assessment form as this will take a long time to discuss. Work out the most appropriate three or four questions which will help the meeting (lasting approximately two hours) to acquire a deeper understanding of the emotional needs of the child.

- Do not carry out the need assessment until the child has been in their placement for six to eight weeks.

- The meeting often views the child as fitting into different aspects of the syndromes of deprivation. It is normal that there should be a variety of thoughts and ideas from professionals in the meeting. The syndrome which brings out the strongest feelings in the meeting about the child is the one to concentrate on for the treatment plan.

- Once the treatment plan is written, a follow-up meeting six to eight weeks later should be held to evaluate progress. The follow-up need assessment should take place three to four months later.

Conclusion

There are now many assessment programmes for children, covering a multitude of complex needs. This chapter has attempted to explain the context of emotional need assessments and how they can help professional workers to reach the lost part of the child, who has been so overwhelmed with unbearable feelings that their sense of hopelessness and helplessness has prevented them from managing the reality of their day-to-day living.

Finally, we need to move away from labelling children, as a defence against our own anxieties. We can find it unbearable to manage children's difficult behaviour when we are working with them. Labelling a child can act as a defence mechanism for the worker. While offering a way of gaining control over their anxieties, it prevents them from developing a deeper insight and understanding about the child's complex needs. The assessment aims to represent a more holistic view of the child's emotional life. The final quotation below offers an insight into the world of the children we are often working with.

Axline (1990) presents the following quote on the back of her book about a little boy named Dibs:

> He would not talk. He would not play. Judged mentally defective, he was oblivious both to other children and to his teacher: in reality he was a brilliant lonely child trapped in a prison of fear and rage, a prison from which only he could release himself.

An emotional need assessment provides a key to unlocking the traumatised child's prison. It is designed to help them find a way of making sense of and relating to their own inner world with a greater confidence and belief in themselves. It allows them to discover a sense of themselves as an individual, making life and external reality more hopeful and meaningful.

CHAPTER 5

THERAPEUTIC TREATMENT PLANS

Putting Them into Practice

Christine Bradley

Introduction

A therapeutic treatment plan is designed to enable workers to create an action plan that enables them to work constructively with unintegrated children. It follows the emotional need assessment and helps to formulate strategies for the provision and support needed for traumatised children who are overwhelmed with unbearable and unthinkable anxieties because of early traumatic experiences. The treatment plan will help workers gain an insight into the child's behaviour, recognising how their current difficulties can be a consequence of a constant reliving of previous traumas. An effective treatment plan will support the child's development in their day-to-day living, helping the 'real self' in the child to evolve. In developing a stronger sense of self, the child will be more able to manage the challenges and realities of the outside world, without breaking down or acting out.

If a treatment plan can be devised during the early stage of the child's placement, it will enable the workers to understand the child's difficult behaviour and respond with insight. Critically, without this insight, a worker can react inappropriately to the behaviour, leaving the child feeling under threat and attacked. This reinforces feelings of panic and rage, which lie embedded in their inner world.

Undertaking a therapeutic treatment plan is not always an easy task for workers, but a crucial step needed to enable and support the child to reach a good outcome during their placement. If a child can allow themselves to accept help and care from their workers for their difficulties, they will move forward from being overwhelmed by feelings of hopelessness and helplessness to expressing ones of hope. It is indeed a major achievement, which is to be valued by both the child and their workers. A successful outcome is reached when the child is in a position to share the world with others and keep to the rules of the community, feeling more at home and comfortable with their own sense of self.

The following passage describes what it means for children to move away from being overwhelmed by feelings of hopelessness and helplessness to accepting enough help to bring about feelings of hope into their lives.

> 'What is real?' asked the Velveteen Rabbit one day. 'Real isn't how you are made,' said the Skin Horse. 'It is a thing which happens to you.' 'Does it hurt?' 'Sometimes,' said the Skin Horse, for he was always truthful. 'When you are real you don't mind being hurt.'
>
> Real is a process that is sometimes intimidating and sometimes painful but in the end far more rewarding than we could ever imagine. (Raiten-d'Antonio 2004:5)

A well-thought-through plan presented to children with meaning can help them to believe that good experiences can happen in the world and they can be real. If they can arrive at this stage of emotional integration with a stronger sense of self, they will be able to make sense of the outside world and, with support, use what is being presented to them positively as they begin to feel more real as a person.

Measuring the outcome

At a recent visit to a children's home where I had been providing consultation about the use of emotional need assessments and therapeutic treatment plans, I met Jane. As I entered the home Jane came over to me and said, 'It's all your fault and I am very angry with you.' I asked her, 'Why?' At this point I was not aware that it was her 14th birthday. She told me that she was not able to go into town, because her worker would be at the staff meeting with me for a part of the day. Thus, she had to stay in the home rather than go to town. I told her that I was terribly sorry to have frustrated her so much and made her feel angry, but I was pleased that she felt able to tell me how she felt. I also explained that there were times in all our lives when we felt let down by those people who were taking care of us. It could be so frustrating, but I was sure that her worker would take her into town later. She smiled at me and said, 'Yes, I know that she will.'

Jane had been in the home for 18 months, and before her placement she had been through several children's home breakdowns, mainly due to her absconding from previous placements or self-harming. After the first three months in her new placement we undertook an emotional need assessment, where she was assessed and identified as functioning within the syndrome of a frozen child with aspects of her day-to-day living at times functioning at the level of an archipelago child. The two syndromes that characterised aspects of Jane's early deprivation revealed that although there were parts of her day-to-day living where she could function and manage stress, there were also other parts which became emotionally frozen. The anxiety and stress that this created could result in parts of her inner world becoming withdrawn and leading to her breaking down and an escalation of destructive acting out.

I realised that the same incident 12 months earlier would have resulted in Jane's feeling of abandonment becoming so powerful because her worker could not take her into town that she would have reacted either by running away or trying to cut herself. At that time, she was unable to communicate the sad or angry feelings that were part of her primitive emotions of panic and rage. An emotional need assessment and therapeutic treatment plan carried out on Jane showed that she needed to feel held in the mind of her workers and have a sense of being nurtured by them. The treatment plan gave workers the tools to provide her with the appropriate provision and support needed to reach a stage of emotional integration during her placement. This enabled her to develop a sense of self which felt sufficiently strong and secure that she could begin to think about her actions and feelings.

A second need assessment was written six months later, investigating the outcome of the first programme. This assessment classified Jane as now functioning at the level of fragile integration; she felt more connected as a person, although she continued to need considerable emotional support and found stress difficult to manage at times, leading her to disintegrate.

My contact with her recently highlighted that because the outcome from the therapeutic treatment plan had been successful she was now able to communicate her feelings. She felt safe enough to trust and share her emotions with others. The current task of the home is to continue to strengthen Jane's level of emotional integration. The aim is that her sense of self and personal identity will begin to focus on her day-to-day living and being, as a person in her own right with a more hopeful view of the outside world. This will enable her to recognise a sense of personal responsibility for herself and others, to take part in a group-living experience, share the world with others and keep to rules.

Monitoring and reviewing the outcome of the need assessment and therapeutic treatment plan is essential in meeting the developing needs of the child. A good outcome of a plan is for the child to feel better about themselves, more supported and provided for by their worker, so that their sense of self has strengthened and they can think about their behaviour, making their life more manageable and bearable. Emotional integration implies that the child's internal world and the external world are working together, creating a sense of self that feels more whole and complete.

What do we expect from a therapeutic treatment plan?

- A greater understanding about meeting the primary and secondary needs of children and adolescents.

- A deeper insight for workers to understand the difficulties these children have when they are managing the challenges of reality that relate back to their early traumatic experiences.

- A recognition of change in the behaviour of the children when they can contain their emotions and the acting out that is more difficult to manage lessens.

- An increase in the quality of communication about feelings of anger and despair between the child and workers.

- The child becomes more aware of their behaviour and the effect it has on others. They can accept personal responsibility for their behaviour, learn from their experiences and make reparation for the damage they have caused to objects and other people.

Meeting of primary needs

The meeting of primary needs represents the maternal and primary provision given to an infant in the early years of their development. If they are traumatised and their primary needs have not been met and provided for, they feel emotionally abandoned by their primary carer. Because they are in the very early stages of their physical and emotional growth, their mentalisation process is also at a very early stage of development. Their anxieties, therefore, are located at a primitive level, not able to be thought through or communicated. If the primary carer does not recognise the child's anxieties, the resulting emotions become embedded in the child's mind. If this is not worked through and dissipated, in later years it recreates their panic and rage, with adverse consequences on the child's development and behaviour.

An older child in adolescence cannot return to being an infant, but a well-planned and structured treatment programme in a therapeutic environment can facilitate the meeting of primary needs. It is possible for the workers to fill in some of the missing gaps of provision from the child's early life, enabling them to feel more emotionally contained and less overwhelmed with unbearable anxieties that they are unable to manage or communicate. The outcome for the worker is to develop a deeper understanding about meeting the child's emotional needs and reduce the child's compulsion to repeat negative behaviour because they feel more contained by the worker.

The primary task is to provide a good experience for the child who did not feel emotionally provided for in their early life through feeding, holding, emotionally containing and nurturing. This takes place at the same time as recognising their maturational age and lack of emotional development, providing for this part of them that has remained stuck in the areas of lost early experiences. The continuity of the provision will help the child to feel a greater emotional integration with a stronger balance between their inner world and meeting the challenges of the external world.

Primary experiences

- *Food.* Unintegrated children often did not experience the provision of food as a good early experience. Workers need to adapt to their primary requirements in terms of food. For example, on returning from their school day, the child can be met by a worker who they depend on with a special drink in a cup, which is their own. The worker needs to spend time with the child in a quiet space while they consume their food or drink and discuss their day and what it has meant to them. This enables the child to make the transition between school and home.

- *Nurturing.* In therapeutic treatment with frozen children there needs to be a part of their day when they experience their workers providing them with a good primary experience of being cared for and nurtured, and the child can allow this to occur and value the experience. This could take place in the morning when the child wakes up, to help them think about the day ahead, or in the evening to help them communicate their anxieties about sleeping and being nurtured. It could be a special blanket, a story being read by the worker, perhaps a toy which could be a transitional object for the child to hold on to and which carries the child's anxieties when they are sleeping. These all reinforce the feeling of being nurtured. It is possible for children at a stage of latency or adolescence to experience a good primary experience when they feel nurtured by their worker.

- *Play.* Unintegrated children are not ready to play and share with other children. It is possible, however, to communicate with frozen children through play. When a suitable structure is provided, they can initiate their own play, often at a tactile level using sand or water and playing with any item they can feel. If adults can continually interact with them in play situations, the child can in time find their own way of playing.

As Tagore wrote:

On the seashore of endless worlds children play. (Tagore 1913)

Meeting of secondary needs

Where a child's primary needs have been met and they feel emotionally nurtured and physically contained by their primary carer, prior to a trauma occurring in their early life, the understanding is that they are moving towards emotional integration. However, when an early traumatic event disrupts their primary attachment and their need for dependency before they are ready to separate, the child becomes emotionally stuck and cannot move into developing emotional integration with a complete sense of self.

If they are abused, their positive feelings about themselves are 'smashed' through and broken down. This leaves the child emotionally 'stuck' in their development and, although functioning at times, they are in danger of disintegrating under the slightest stress. It can become too difficult for them to make a natural transition from absolute dependence through to interdependence. They begin to present as a separate person (a false self) away from their real self, who continues to be dependent on their carer. They become pseudo-independent, leaving the false self to look after them before they are ready to do so (Dockar-Drysdale 1990). To survive, they develop strategies that can prevent them from managing the demands of aspects of reality in their life. At times, they become emotionally fragile because they do not hold sufficient emotional resources to contain themselves. Without support from their workers they can easily break down.

Children who did have their primary needs met for a substantial period of their early life have been through a good primary experience. This gives them a feeling of being a person in their own right. However, they need emotional support from their carers if their maturational growth and development are to continue. When functioning breaks down, workers need to be aware that support is needed through the difficult periods in their life.

The primary task of meeting secondary needs: ego support and ego provision

The task here is to support children to build up their emotional resources and levels of ego functioning, strengthening their sense of self and personal identity and helping them to accept personal responsibility for their actions.

Workers should develop awareness about variations in the children's functioning to help them work through aspects of the day when they are in danger of disintegrating and returning to a period where they may not have felt emotionally contained by the primary carer. The result of meeting children's primary needs when they become emotionally fragile is that their level of functioning becomes stronger and more creative as their belief in themselves is stronger and more meaningful.

The following part of the chapter presents a therapeutic treatment plan for each syndrome of deprivation discussed earlier.

The treatment plan

Undertaking a therapeutic treatment plan provides workers with appropriate tools to prevent them from over-identifying with the child's false self, and reaches beyond to the 'lost child' who has locked themselves away in their inner world feeling abandoned and emotionally remote from the rest of the world. The treatment plan provides a model for workers to help them to provide the child with elements of primary and secondary experiences, which they did not receive in their early years.

Table 5.1: Treatment plan for the frozen child

The frozen child

The child requires the provision of good primary experiences, which are consistent, in a well-structured and thought-out setting. The worker needs to become attuned to the child, holding them in their mind.

Frozen children remain at the stage of pre-attachment. Their primary experiences were inconsistent and did not help the infant to feel held in their carer's mind and emotionally contained. Instead, they felt overwhelmed by their sense of abandonment. Their inner world became frozen, and they were unable to reach out to others. In their developing years, they either became emotionally isolated, cut off from the rest of the world, or they disrupted the functioning of other children. If workers are to help them to unfreeze and express their emotional needs, the following two areas of therapeutic work need to be addressed.

Emotional containment

The frozen child is not able to contain themselves and hold on to their internal boundaries, and is consequently more likely to disrupt reality and break through the external boundaries placed on them by adults. Frozen children have often found the outside world so hostile and painful that they develop their own reality for which they create the rules. Their workers and carers need to be able to help them to understand the rules of the outside world and how to manage these. If the frozen child is to become more emotionally contained, they need to reach a dependency with their worker whose practice is informed by the treatment plan.

Absolute dependence

A frozen child did not experience a sense of absolute dependence in their early years. Therefore, when they do attach to their workers they recreate their need for a primary merger, when two people become one. Having not yet reached a stage of two people attaching, once they do attach, they merge to become a part of that other person. Workers need to be aware that, as a frozen child begins to depend on them, they must ensure that the child knows that they are being held in mind, and the workers must understand that separation is too difficult for the child to manage.

cont.

Questions	Explanations and actions
Does the child merge and disrupt the functioning of others?	**Explanation:** Frozen children cannot manage boundaries; they find group experiences very difficult because of their need to merge with an individual. Consequently, they will disrupt the functioning of others.
	Action: The frozen child can only function as part of a group if they have an adult with them. If good primary experiences are provided for them continually, they can develop a strong sense of absolute dependence on their worker. Because of the continuity of the relationship, their sense of self will strengthen sufficiently to the point where they will be able to engage in group experiences and adhere to agreed rules.
Can the child contain emotions or do they act out violently when under stress?	**Explanation:** Frozen children cannot manage emotions; their sense of self-esteem is so low they place no value on themselves. Therefore, they find it very difficult to think about their feelings. Reaction from their workers can lead to their panic and rage 'exploding' and being acted out.
	Action: The child needs constant encouragement from you. If they have been positive in their actions, let them know how much their actions and achievements are valued. It is important for you to recognise how difficult it is for the child to value themselves. If they can be aware that you recognise their painful feelings, it will help them to continue to function, and to realise that you are prepared to take care of them until they can look after themselves.
Does the child show any evidence of using survival techniques to protect themselves from the pressures of reality?	**Explanation:** If a child becomes manic in their behaviour, their energy is out of control and they make workers feel anxious and worried about them. It is a sign they are overwhelmed with anxieties, which they are out of touch with, and are in denial of their emotions. To survive they have built a wall around themselves, which makes them difficult to access as they are so cut off and out of touch with reality. At times, their fantasy world can take over from the reality they do not want to acknowledge.
	Action: A *survival* mechanism is not a way of helping the child to cope with anxiety. It is mainly a reaction to unbearable and unthinkable feelings. A healthy *defence* mechanism helps to reduce anxiety in the child as they are protecting their sense of self.
	If the child leaves you feeling anxious or worried about them, let them know that you have been thinking about them since you last met. The fact that you were left feeling concerned about them suggests to you that perhaps they are feeling horrible about themselves. Say you wonder if there is any way you could help them prior to them feeling they can no longer control themselves.

Is the child able to communicate their fears and anxieties, either in a non-verbal or verbal way? Are the workers able to understand and interpret the child's acting out appropriately, to enable them to articulate the despair that leads them to panic?	**Explanation:** Frozen children are not able to communicate through words at the beginning of their therapeutic treatment. Their trauma occurred at a pre-verbal stage of their development. **Action:** Create as many opportunities as possible for the child to communicate at a non-verbal and symbolic level. Using too many words could make them feel attacked. Remember, acting out can be a breakdown of communication, which needs to be understood and addressed. You could undertake training to understand more about non-verbal communication and the role of symbolic communication in working practice and converting symbols into words, helping the child to express themselves.
Does the child show that they can learn from experience and the consequences of their actions?	**Explanation:** Frozen children find it difficult to learn emotionally and intellectually from experience. Their fear of breakdown is high. They need one adult to be engaged with them at both a logical and intuitive level. **Action:** The child needs one-to-one help. Be aware of their emotional rawness and fear of breakdown. Support them by helping their challenges of learning through small, simple and manageable stages. They need to be aware that you are prepared to learn with them.
Has the child ever learned how to play?	**Explanation:** A frozen child can find it very difficult to play on their own with pleasure. They did not have a meaningful play experience with their primary carer, nor did they feel emotionally contained by them. They continue to seek the need for primary experience in their play. **Action:** The child needs opportunities for sensory play. Whatever their age they could benefit from receiving some good primary play experiences, including: play with puppets; storytelling; and reading books or writing stories with each other or with a person who they feel emotionally contained by and who can survive their need to annihilate their play (McMahon 1992). They need to have a reliable time each day when they play with a specific adult, who they can depend on, using their play opportunities in ways that can help their emotional development.

■ CASE STUDY: ABSOLUTE DEPENDENCE AND HOLDING IN MIND OF THE FROZEN CHILD

Matthew was a 12-year-old boy who had been placed in a children's home for six months. The placement followed several breakdowns in other homes due to his aggressive behaviour. He had reached the stage in his current placement where he was beginning to attach and become dependent on one worker. As part of my work with the staff team, I was in the process of explaining the emotional rawness in frozen children and how they could easily feel abandoned by their workers. They find separation very difficult to manage. The simplest experience of loss brings out primitive emotions, originating from early childhood anxiety and potentially resulting in extreme acting out.

At this point, Matthew's worker whom he was starting to become dependent on became quite anxious and told me that she was about to embark on a long-planned holiday and would be away for two-and-a-half weeks. Would that make him feel abandoned by her? I replied that this was a real possibility, but there was a way of working around this. I suggested that before she left for her holiday, she should write him several short letters letting him know that she was thinking about him, and one would be given to him each evening by another worker. These letters given to him while she was away would remind him that she would be returning to see him shortly. When she did return to her work Matthew ran to her showing his delight to see her and letting her know how much he enjoyed his letters from her. Their work continued as it was before she went on her holiday. Matthew continued to remain absolutely dependent on her until, eventually, he could attach to other workers and enjoy the group activities in the home. Without the letters she left for Matthew, he could have felt that his worker was not going to return, providing another experience of emotional abandonment, which he had repeatedly experienced in his early years. This had resulted in his sense of panic and rage being acted out while he remained in a frozen state of unintegration.

Some time after this, Matthew achieved a sufficient level of emotional integration to enable him to be successfully fostered.

Table 5.2: Treatment plan for the archipelago child

The archipelago child

This child has had the benefit of some good experiences from their primary carer. However, these experiences did not continue sufficiently for them to have developed enough emotional security to move to the next stage, through a natural transition. Instead, the child was left with a degree of panic and rage inside them, which at times of stress could prevent them from functioning. An archipelago child has been described as a scattering of islands with large gaps of water in between in which you can either drown or find a way of swimming through. The child is at times able to function and manage their daily living circumstances. However, because their traumas occurred at such an early stage before the development of thought and language and were later compounded with further traumas, the resulting emotions of anger and sadness became embedded in the developing brain. Workers need to be aware of the archipelago child's emotional fragility, recognising that without the support of the worker they can break down and begin to act out destructively. The following areas need to be addressed when working with archipelago children.

Separation and loss managing transitions

A child who experienced separation and loss prematurely has not yet acquired sufficient emotional resources and belief in themselves to adapt to and think with interest about the outside world. Although they experienced a level of absolute dependency on their primary carer, they lost it before they were ready to make a natural transition to the secondary stage of their development, where they could build the necessary defence mechanisms to protect themselves. Instead, they continue to survive unbearable feelings of separation and loss through the development of a false self, which if challenged can lead to breakdown in their day-to-day living.

In a healthy early mother–child relationship, children often begin to give up their need for absolute dependence by using a transitional object (such as a blanket or teddy bear). Internalising their early experiences helps them to manage the next stage of their journey into external reality. Where a child does not make use of a transitional object to enable them to reach a stage of separation and interdependence with their primary carer, it is likely that their belief in themselves is limited. Without support from their carers, they find separation and stressful situations difficult to manage.

Functioning and non-functioning

Children who can continue to function under stress maintain a stronger sense of self in their inner world. With support, they can hold on to their sense of purpose, perform a task and see it through to completion. They can also think about their actions and the impact of their sometimes difficult-to-manage behaviour on others.

To help children to continue to function they need ongoing ego support. Non-functioning implies that their sense of self-esteem has become very limited. Their behaviour becomes impulse driven and they cannot think about their actions or learn from them. Reality seems so unbearable that they cease to function because they feel attacked by it and plan to attack back. To help non-functioning children to function, the worker needs to support them with good primary experiences. In this instance, the archipelago child needs considerable ego provision to help them through their emotionally fragile state until they can begin to strengthen and function again.

cont.

Questions	Explanations and actions
Does the child have several areas of functioning? Is help needed when functioning breaks down, or can the child manage stress and transition?	**Explanation:** An archipelago child has a basis of emotional resources to function positively for a short period. However, there are certain circumstances when they become overwhelmed with the pressure of meeting the challenges of reality in their daily life. Where their childhood traumas were interspersed with good experiences from their carer when they felt emotionally nurtured by them, they carry a mixed bag of emotions. This can lead them to move from a period of feeling positive and hopeful about their growth and development emotionally and intellectually, to times when their inner world becomes overwhelmed with despair, hopelessness and helplessness. Their sense of self is still fragmented as they have not yet reached a sense of becoming a whole person and an individual in their own right. **Action:** Be careful not to idealise them when they are functioning and expect this to continue indefinitely. When their functioning does break down, it is important not to express disappointment to them; respond but do not react. When their functioning diminishes, this could be the time when they require structured primary provision from you.
Does the child act out violently when under stress?	**Explanation:** When the archipelago child is functioning well, stressful factors in their lives can be expressed through anger and sadness, but when they cease to function it is more difficult to manage their emotions. Their anger and sadness can turn into panic and rage, which they cannot contain and which can be acted out violently when reacted to by their worker. **Action:** Help the child to realise that they recognise how difficult and painful they are finding it to manage their current difficulties. Provide them with an experience at a primary level, which will help them to feel looked after rather than emotionally abandoned.

Does the child show any evidence of self-harming or suicidal gestures? Are they aware of the onset of these occurrences?	**Explanation:** When an archipelago child's emotional life becomes unbearable they can disintegrate. Their self-esteem weakens and they are 'locked into' their own sense of despair and hopelessness. This leads them to acting out self-destructive behaviour. Their sense of self feels threatened and they attempt to destroy anything that felt positive in their life. The child falls into their own inner world 'black hole'.
	Action: Remain in touch with the child when they begin to show a deep sense of anxiety, which is becoming unbearable. At this stage, it is important not to react to them as this will feed into their fear of being attacked by the outside world, leading them to act out. Let them know that you are aware they are worrying about themselves. Suggest that perhaps you should both find a quiet space where you can sit down with a drink and biscuit to talk about what is making them feel so terrible. Then you can think about a way in which you can help them to feel better. Ensuring that they know that you are in touch with some of their own unbearable feelings will make them feel a little more hopeful about their current difficulties.
Can the child communicate their fears and anxieties to any degree or do they distance themselves when anxious or distressed?	**Explanation:** The archipelago child can communicate with support when they are functioning. When they begin to cease functioning and are emotionally disintegrating, they can neither communicate their feelings nor find the words needed to express their fears and anxieties. They do not have the words to express themselves when they cannot feel emotions. At the point of breakdown, they move from idealising themselves to denigrating their sense of self, and towards acting out destructively or self-destructively.
	Action: Provide many opportunities for them to communicate symbolically. Use stories or painting to provide them with creative ways to communicate. If you can stay with the children's despair and self-destructiveness, you protect them from their more primitive impulses and their emotions feel less raw. As their sense of self begins to develop again they will be more able to communicate through words about how they feel.

cont.

Questions	Explanations and actions
Does the child show that they can learn from experience and the consequences of their actions?	**Explanation:** When the archipelago child is functioning, they can learn from their experiences emotionally or intellectually. However, when they disintegrate and fall into their own dark hole, losing their belief in themselves, they cease to learn. As they believe that all past experiences of trauma will be repeated if they fail, they begin to act out and repeat previous behaviours. **Action:** The child needs one-to-one help. You need to be aware of the pain and despair the child can reach if they continue to repeat past experiences. Identify how long they can be expected to function in a challenging situation. Ensure that your expectation of what they can achieve is presented to them in small stages, building up to a point where they are ready to undertake more challenges.
Is the child's play easily distracted and sometimes destructive?	**Explanation:** The archipelago child is characterised as having small islets of functioning in their inner world. Consequently, their sense of self can fall apart under stress. They can find playing with others in a group difficult, and will attempt to disrupt its cohesion. To bring the fragmented parts of their world together through play, they need play experiences designed to help them feel more whole as a person. From this they can then move towards social play and sharing their world with others. The sense of self of the archipelago child is so fragmented they need to engage in play that reflects early stages of development. **Action:** They need opportunities for transitional play using a cloth, a toy or a blanket, which provides the child with a sense of protection from the outside world. With the use of a transitional object, the child can move forwards to the use of symbolism in their play stories, drawing and music. It is through these types of play experiences that the archipelago child may be able to communicate and relate to their fears and anxieties – 'the transitional object supports the child engaged in the perpetual human task of keeping inner and outer reality separate yet interrelated' (Winnicott 1971:2).

■ CASE STUDY: BRINGING TOGETHER THE INTERNAL AND EXTERNAL REALITIES OF THE ARCHIPELAGO CHILD

Kate was a 14-year-old girl who was placed in her third children's home. She had had some good and positive experiences as a small child with a close relationship with her father and one other person. She had also been overwhelmed by significant painful and traumatic experiences through the death of siblings, and had a strong sense of emotional abandonment from her mother and other carers. She did not feel emotionally contained. Her inner world was full of unbearable and unthinkable anxieties, which were expressed through panic and rage acted out towards others. Such behaviour was the reason for previous placement breakdowns. An emotional need assessment on Kate identified her as functioning at the level of an archipelago child. She had levels of functioning (based on the good experiences she had as a child) with gaps in her emotional life that led to any stress factors returning her to non-functioning periods. The three questions which were discussed when undertaking the need assessment programme on Kate were: boundaries, containing anxiety, anger and stress, and communication. The overall view of Kate's assessment was that although with support she could function as a 14-year-old girl, at other times she reverted to behaving like a lost three-year-old. At this point, she needed to feel held in the mind of her workers until she could manage her current reality. When she was at the stage of behaving like a three-year-old, Kate could easily feel attacked by the outside world, leading her to behave destructively. Workers realised that it was important to respond to her emotional age until she could manage her current reality without anxiety.

Kate was full of powerful and violent emotions, which she slowly became more aware of. To cope with her emotional fragility, which was at times quite raw, she would either idealise herself or remain in denial about how terrible she felt. She found it difficult to communicate through words, but with help from her workers became more able to express anxieties by using words symbolically. I suggested to her worker that perhaps they should write a story together. Kate said that she would like that idea and so they began.

Worker: Once upon a time there was a little girl standing in a room with lots of people. One grown-up in the room said, 'Isn't she like an angel.' Suddenly the little girl started throwing all her toys on the floor. The grown-up said, 'Why have you thrown all your toys on the floor?'

Kate: Because they called me an angel and I do not like angels.

Worker: But to be an angel means that there are lots of good things inside you.

Kate: But there are no good things inside me.

Worker: But you have, we must help you find them.

Kate: How do I find the starting point?

Worker: We are going to help you to find the starting point.

Over the following year, the worker helped to bring both parts of Kate together, the three-year-old and the adolescent. The part of Kate that was a traumatised three-year-old asked for a special drink each evening, which was given to her in her own cup. When she was ill it was their opportunity to take care of her like a small child. This provision was delivered while also supporting the 14-year-old in Kate to find a way of helping her sad and angry feelings, which were represented by the angels and devils, to live together facing the ups and downs that life incurred.

Workers continued to stay with her and emotionally contain her panic and despair until she began to feel more settled and not so controlled by her own primitive impulses. This drew her areas of functioning and non-functioning together, prior to her moving to a more independent living arrangement when she was ready for the move. She had been continuing to write her story, and prior to her move Kate wrote: 'I have now found the new starting point and the right road to begin walking down, but I find it difficult to move from being very unhappy to being happy in one minute.' Her worker replied, 'If you can survive your doldrums Kate, there are times when you will feel miserable, but you must realise that knowing about your own misery can lead to you feeling better about yourself.' Kate replied, 'Even if there is a thunderstorm, it will finish and the sun will come out again and the flowers will start to grow.' Throughout the story, Kate was describing the dark and stormy areas in her inner world and how they had begun to come together during the therapeutic treatment she received at the home. By using the programme, the missing parts of her inner world had begun to come together. Kate had now reached the stage of emotional integration, ready to embark on a placement of semi-independence and beginning to take personal responsibility for herself and her actions.

Table 5.3: Treatment plan for the caretaker child

The caretaker child

The concept of the caretaker self is explained by Winnicott as the significance of the infant's primary relationship with the mother, father or alternative carer. Although in a state of maternal preoccupation with the infant, the carer is unable to empathise with the infant's emotional needs. Therefore, they cannot offer the necessary ego provision and support required to develop and strengthen the infant's sense of self while they are developing. To survive their emotional turbulence the infant begins to build up their own defences at a very early stage in their development. To hold on to themselves without breaking down or acting out, the infant has to build up and become their own 'caretaker' self, because there is no other person to emotionally contain them. The real self never develops since, 'without the initial good-enough environmental provision, the feeling of being real is absent and if there is too much chaos, the ultimate feeling is of futility. Inherent difficulties of life cannot be reached, let alone satisfied' (Abram 1996:189).

The caretaker child does receive bits of good experiences, becoming absolutely dependent on a primary carer. However, the dependency does not become sufficiently established for the infant to make a positive transition from the carer to the first 'not-me' relationship, so that they can move towards meaningful attachment relationships. The key to therapeutic work with the child is to help them reach a stage where they can hand the caretaker part of their self to the worker, whom they trust. They can express the real self who feels lost and abandoned, needing to feel nurtured and looked after. If the worker becomes the caretaker, this allows the child's real self to feel looked after, becoming attached to an object or a form of provision. It is important that the dependency on the provision continues, enabling the real self to emotionally develop and grow, moving towards emotional integration and attachment relationships. In terms of the syndromes of deprivation, the caretaker self is towards the border of emotional integration, having received some good primary experiences but having lost them prematurely. The hope is that they can be found and put back together again. With appropriate therapeutic treatment, the real self begins to grow, feeling more real and linked in with other parts of their sense of self. Thus, the child moves towards emotional integration and coming together as a whole person. A sign of maturation is when they no longer need to be a 'caretaker'. They feel stronger with their own sense of self and relationships becoming more real and meaningful.

cont.

Questions	Explanations and actions
When under stress does the child merge and disrupt the functioning of others?	**Explanation:** Under stress, a caretaker child attempts to take control of the group rather than disrupt it. This child is a caretaker in charge of their own little self, and this drives them to control the rest of the group setting and its members. Although they do not disrupt the group, this powerful need to control can prevent the group members from continuing to function. **Action:** Let the child know that although you do understand why they must be so controlling, it would be more helpful if they allowed you to take care of them, as you are aware that they are very anxious and worried. You become the caretaker, leaving the child to be the little self who needs looking after.
Does the child act out violently when under stress or when feeling under threat?	**Explanation:** The caretaker child under stress is more likely to have temper tantrums, like a two- or three-year-old. Rather than panic and rage, their inner world is consumed with feelings of anger and sadness. Under pressure and abreaction, their anger can turn to violence and rage, but with support it can be worked through. **Action:** A caretaker child is more able to accept personal responsibility for their actions than children who are deeply unintegrated. When you notice that the pressure is building up inside the child, you need to let the child know that you are aware they are becoming anxious and unsure about themselves. Suggest that you find a quiet space where you both can sit and talk about how the child is feeling.
Does the child have a strong sense of self-preservation or is it haphazard?	**Explanation:** The caretaker child does have a sense of self, but the real self functions as a 'little self' who wants to be taken care of. Their sense of self can at times strengthen, but is still fragile, and under stress can fall apart. **Action:** You need to help the child to hand the caretaker over to you to be looked after, and to provide for the little self who needs to be taken care of. At this point, the provision of good experience being adapted to meet their primary needs for a short period of the day becomes important. For example, a cuddly toy they can communicate with, a drink or special food. There is a part of their self which continues to feel emotionally contained by you, until they acknowledge that they no longer require the provision.

Is the child able to communicate symbolically rather than verbally?	**Explanation:** Caretaker children can communicate verbally to a degree, but their real and meaningful communication is often at a symbolic level.
	Action: Offer as many creative opportunities as possible for them to symbolically communicate, including drama, story writing, poetry, painting and music. This allows the symbols to become the third object of communication, making it easier for the children to eventually find words to express themselves.
Does the child find learning at school a difficult experience?	**Explanation:** The child finds the school situation with its order and boundaries difficult to adhere to. It is easier to gain control of the classroom setting themselves, rather than functioning under the rules and regulations of the school. They feel vulnerable and can pick this up in others. The teacher or carer needs to become the responsive caretaker to the little self until they can accept and recognise the child's need to function and learn.
	Action: The child requires a one-to-one situation to help them to want to learn. There is the potential to learn, but they need a great deal of emotional support to believe that you (in the form of an adult or teacher) can take care of their little self, thereby increasing their desire to learn.
Can the child play creatively and symbolically to communicate their inner world and current sense of self, or do they remain fixated at an earlier stage of their development?	**Explanation:** Caretaker children can play by themselves and with others. They can be creative in their functioning and at times use their playfulness to manage the reality of the outside world.
	Action: Ensure that they have several play opportunities at both an infantile and chronological level, since their play must represent opportunities for them to communicate and to be creative.

■ CASE STUDY: TOM 'EEKING' OUT AN EXISTENCE. THE CREATIVE USE OF SYMBOLIC COMMUNICATION WITH CARETAKER CHILDREN

Tom had the ability to get under everyone's skin. He made constant demands of his workers by either screeching into their faces or tugging their clothes. He needed them to be totally preoccupied with him to help him survive his overwhelming feelings. His teacher described him as having no beginning and no centre to his sense of being a person; bits of him were scattered everywhere. Under stress he became manic, turning cartwheels over and over again, rather like a ball of wool where the beginning has become lost in the middle. Tom was an unintegrated child; his behaviour was so disruptive he would upset group happenings and not allow others to function at mealtimes or in the classroom setting; he was constantly being moved from group situations.

Tom's symbolic way of communicating was through a consistent 'Eek'. This was not through a word, more a constant squeaking. His need to express himself was so powerful it prevented the classroom lesson from functioning. I advised his teacher Jo not to ask Tom to leave the classroom because of his noise, as this would compound his feeling of emotional abandonment. They should suggest to Tom that he should place 'Eek', who by that time was symbolised by a troll doll, on the empty desk in the classroom, to allow 'Eek' to stay with him and let him feel that he was being thought about. Tom was delighted at not being sent out of the classroom. He brought 'Eek' in the following morning and placed him on the desk. He sat himself down and for the rest of the school day did not disrupt the class with his eeking and squeaking, and he began to learn. The teacher was delighted with his response and how it changed the dynamics of the classroom setting. 'Eek' symbolised the little self in Tom, who had felt lost and abandoned. Keeping him in the classroom helped Tom to feel that he did not have to be the 'caretaker' as the teacher had taken over that role. In time, Tom did so well in the classroom setting that he was moved to a higher class. Eventually, as he became more emotionally integrated, he was fostered. Before he left he went back to Jo's classroom and asked her if she would take care of 'Eek', as he was leaving and thought that he still needed to be taken care of. She said that she would. One year later Tom returned to see her and said that she no longer needed to take care of 'Eek', as he was settled where he was. Jo told him that she was delighted he was settled, and said that she would place 'Eek' in the cupboard where he would be happy.

This case study illustrates how important it is for workers to recognise and respond to the little self in the caretaker child, who often communicates at a symbolic level. If the child can acknowledge that their workers recognise and wish to reach out to the lost and abandoned part of their real self, this will help them to understand how the outside world and their inner world can relate to one another with a sense of coherence.

The emotionally fragile integrated child

A child who is developing towards reaching the level of ego integration through the treatment and provision received from their carers has acquired a sense of self that has become strong enough to examine and explore the realities of the outside world. In experiencing a sense of emotional containment, they now want to look for something outside themselves, becoming interested in moving towards a sense of self-discovery. Having acquired a sense of self and 'being', which they feel comfortable with, they are now able to progress to what Winnicott called 'doing'. This is in contrast with primitive agonies and unthinkable anxieties, which continue to dominate the inner world of the unintegrated child (Abram 1996). The emotionally integrated child has now reached the stage of having the capacity and emotional resources to make meaningful attachments with their carers, because they experience themselves as a person in their own right. Although at times they can become very fragile and disintegrate, with help and support from their carers they can come back together again, continuing to develop emotionally. With a growing sense of self, reality can be thought about and, with support from their carers, worked with and managed.

Winnicott (1990:54) describes integration as the establishment of a unit of self, writing, 'It can be said that good enough ego coverage (provision) by the mother (in respect of their unthinkable anxieties) enables the new human person to build up a personality on the pattern of a continuity of going-on-being.' In this, he explains that if the primary provision needed in the early experiences of the infant is missed out on, but later provided for by their workers, it can enable them to develop and strengthen their sense of self, feeling strong enough to continue with 'going-on-being' and more prepared to make sense of and manage the external reality.

Dockar-Drysdale (1990) wrote that a child's view of reality was dependent on their inner world and, where this was peopled by tormenting devils and raging monsters, the outer reality would be seen as a threatening and terrible place. We cannot take away the inner turmoil and unbearable anxieties that children and young people carry with them because of their early traumatic experiences. But by creating an environment that can meet their emotional needs, we can help them begin to internalise the good experiences provided for them, and to come together as a person who is more able to think about and express their painful emotions. Learning how to carry on being a person without breaking down will lead them to a growing realisation that a good experience can be internalised. Satisfying relationships can be achieved and continued. Integration is related to health and an ability to be, subsequent to doing: 'There is also the ability to distinguish between their Me and Not-me situations, and think about what is outside and inside their own sense of self' (Abram 1996:68).

Depression

As a child becomes more emotionally integrated, life begins to feel better and more hopeful for them with their carers or workers. However, with a greater awareness of self, it can also become more painful and difficult to understand why they have these unbearable feelings of loss and grief. Childhood depression affects many children and is characterised by feelings of guilt and a sense of worthlessness, a lack of zest for life, self-accusations and frequent suicidal thoughts and impulses (Trowell 2011). Winnicott (1978) saw depression as a wide concept, ranging from a near-normal state to near psychotic.

With an emotionally integrated child, the depression exists but can be thought about, and the underlying conflict resolved and worked through with support and help from their carers, workers or therapists. In therapeutic work with integrated children, we can view depression as a sign of hope, as they become more in touch with their inner-world experiences. With a great amount of appropriate support and work with their carers, the child can find opportunities to work through their loss and grief from previous traumas. They can continue to build up an emotional strength to develop meaningful attachment relationships, finding their place in reality, which is manageable and bearable for them.

Table 5.4: The fragile integrated child

Key questions	Explanation
Can the child hold on to boundaries, but pushes them in an anti-authority way?	A fragile integrated child has a greater awareness about the importance of boundaries than unintegrated children. Under stress, they are more likely to challenge and become anti-authority as they begin to accept personal responsibility for their actions and be part of a group. Their ability to manage boundaries influences the group dynamic. Either they can help the group to function or during their own stressful periods can disrupt and prevent it from functioning.
Do they disintegrate when very anxious and are they unable to talk about stress?	Although the sense of self in the fragile integrated child is stronger than it is in the other syndromes of deprivation, they can manage stress factors only for a short period. Their emotional resources are not yet strong enough to hold on to their self-esteem continually. When they fall apart and disintegrate, with support from their workers they will come back together again and begin to communicate about their anxieties and uncertainties.
Under stress, do they lack self-esteem and become self-destructive?	As stated above, they can lose their developing self-esteem. It is important to remain aware when they appear to become emotionally fragile. Let them know that you are aware that the challenge they are having to face can be difficult and painful for them. Help them to maintain a level of value and awareness about what they have achieved. For a brief period, they may need to know that their worker is going to take care of them until they can return to taking care of themselves. Help them to see that they do not need to revert to their earlier self-destructive behaviour. They will then begin to work through the emotions that have begun to feel quite unbearable for them and continue to function.

cont.

Key questions	Explanation
Is communication at a more symbolic level with investment in verbal communication? Do they find it difficult to face reality when communication breaks down?	Fragile integrated children can communicate symbolically. They are reaching the stage of emotional development where they can begin to express themselves verbally, but require some help with their communication. At this stage, they will be ready to use therapy. Workers need to remain aware of the level of their communication and the point at which they cease to communicate. Remember that many of their unbearable feelings have not been communicated before, so it will take them time to begin to use language to express their emotions. If they cease to communicate they can be in danger of acting out their emotions.
Does the child have a general commitment to school and the experiences offered to them?	Fragile integrated children are either committed to learning or resistant to being taught. This depends on the dynamics of the classroom influencing the sense of security the child has within the setting. Fragile integrated children are in a stage of transition from being without a sense of personal responsibility with a lack of guilt and concern, to focusing more on a sense of doing and learning, and making reparation for their destructive behaviour. Stress can result in them returning to their points of breakdown when they were unintegrated. A child who is working towards a level of ego development and a strengthening sense of self is now able to think about the stress they are under and needs opportunities to communicate with their workers about their difficulties. Responding sensitively towards them helps them to reflect about what the learning experience means. As they begin to realise what they can gain from their learning environment, it will help them to take in the experience and link in more positively with the reality they are working with.
Does the child engage in solitary or co-operative play?	A child at the stage of fragile integration is more able to play with others and keep to the rules, although at times they need more symbolic and creative play. Play can be used as a greater form of imagination with them, projecting and working through some of their more painful feelings and memories. Children at the stage of ego integration begin to differentiate between fantasy and reality. They can use their play environment to work through some of the difficulties they experience when balancing the realities of their external and internal worlds.

Action plans for fragile integrated children

The following four areas are central to therapeutic work with fragile integrated children:

Personal responsibility

As the child moves towards integration, their sense of self begins to strengthen and they build up a greater awareness of their actions. The attachment relationship between the worker and child develops, enabling them to acquire a sense of reliability and trustworthiness about their actions. As the child begins to come together as a person, with help and support they can start to hold greater accountability for their behaviour and gain control over their actions. The worker must focus on the child's personal identity and sense of self, helping them to achieve a greater sense of personal responsibility.

Disintegration

As the child begins to come together as a person, they are not yet emotionally strong enough to consistently manage difficult and painful experiences in their day-to-day living. If the pressure of the outside world feels too much for them, they begin to view the outside world as a dangerous and threatening place to be, and start to feel attacked by it. They retreat to their inner world and are in danger of disintegrating and returning to their point of breakdown. Workers should respond sensitively and thoughtfully to them, helping them not to give up on their ego-developmental process. It's important to stress that an episode of disintegration will lead to a coming together, which could make them feel stronger.

Communication

Offer as many opportunities as possible for the child to communicate, particularly about the stress of managing reality. Support them to invest in their level of communication when they are trying to face their challenges. Follow the level of their communication, as acting out of difficult behaviour is likely to occur if communication diminishes. Always remain in touch with their quality of communication. Express your concerns when you view it as breaking down, and ask them if you can help them in any way. At the level of fragile integration, the child still needs to know that they are held in mind.

Transference and counter-transference

As the child begins to feel like a person with their own sense of self, they start to transfer some of their emotions, which arise from experiences and traumas with previous figures in their lives, on to their workers. To counter this, the worker needs to have an in-depth understanding of the dynamics of transference and counter-transference in order to work effectively with the child. (Refer to the glossary for explanations of transference and counter-transference.)

▇ CASE STUDY: THE ABILITY TO ACCEPT PERSONAL RESPONSIBILITY FOR ACTIONS AND THE NEED FOR EGO SUPPORT

Carole was a 14-year-old girl who was placed in a children's home after a period of stay in a secure unit and several placement breakdowns. An emotional need assessment was carried out after she had been in her current placement for a few months. Although Carole had had some good early experiences as a small child, she had also been subjected to turbulent and traumatic events. Her early attachment relationships had broken down before she was ready to make a natural transition from her primary carer to becoming less dependent on them. Consequently, as a result of these experiences, Carole was overwhelmed with feelings of hostility and fears of abandonment which she acted out by merging and over-identifying with the anti-social tendency of drug and alcohol abuse. The emotional need assessment identified her as functioning at the level of a 'caretaker self'. At that time, Carole was not able to learn from her experiences. Her self-esteem was very low, although she presented as being in control of her actions. Workers also became aware of the part of Carole that constantly felt like a small child who expected painful and terrible situations in her life; either these would occur or she would create them. The caretaker self represented the part of Carole who from an early age had learned to look after herself, with a lost part of her which remained 'stuck' at an early age of her developmental process.

Over the following year with the insight and understanding her workers had gained about the therapeutic work needed from them as a result of her emotional need assessment, Carole began to express her anxieties and concerns to them. The continuity of the workers' presence in her life and an awareness that they were thinking about her and holding her in their mind helped her to feel secure enough with them to express her vulnerability. The second need assessment on Carole showed that her emotional maturational process had developed enough for her to be assessed as being on the level of an integrated child. Although still quite emotionally fragile at times, her sense of self was becoming stronger, feeling more alive. The example below illustrates this.

A member of staff, to whom Carole had become attached, was leaving; this was her first experience of a worker's departure since her arrival at the home two years earlier. The day she was leaving, Carole also had an argument with a friend on her mobile phone. The combination of these two stress factors was too much for Carole to manage, and she became overwhelmed with panic and rage. As a result, Carole kicked the television set in the home and broke the screen. After her outrage had been worked through with the help and support of her workers, she was able to accept personal responsibility for her actions, explaining that she was furious with her friend and angry and upset that her worker was leaving; it had all been too much for her. She apologised for her actions and was able to accept that she would have to pay a small amount to help with the repair of the television. With help and support from her special worker she was also able to work through the impact of the separation from her and how it had brought up feelings for her about previous separations in her life.

Previously Carole would not have been able to accept personal responsibility for her actions and continued to be destructive or self-harming. This is a good example of emotional integration, described as the coming together of a person who can accept the reality of the external world. Carole is planning to move into her own semi-independent provision and feels ready to make such a transition, but is also able to communicate her fears and anxieties about the future. She is now in a position where the main focus of the therapeutic treatment plan for her future is about the level of ego support she needs from those working with her. Carole has achieved a sense of self, which although fragile has strengthened, and she carries a greater belief in herself as an individual.

Conclusion

This chapter discussed the insight and understanding needed from workers and carers if therapeutic work with children and young people is to be successful. It focused on outlining the therapeutic task required in the management of children and young people whose assessment programme identifies the level of their emotional needs that were not provided for in their early years.

The therapeutic task is a long and arduous one for workers, if they are to enable the child's sense of self to strengthen and deepen to the point where they can manage the outside world without breaking down. Donald Winnicott stated:

> It may be a kind of loving, but often it is a kind of hating, and the key word is not treatment or cure but rather it is survival. If you survive, then the child has a chance to grow and become something like the person he or she would have been if the untoward environmental breakdown had not brought disaster. (Winnicott 1997:228)

My years of experience tell me that workers can bear the most unbearable aspects of a child's behaviour by using insight gained from a conceptual understanding of the therapeutic care and treatment needed. In this way, the potential outcome for the child or young person becomes more positive.

CHAPTER 6

CREATING A THERAPEUTIC CULTURE

Christine Bradley

Introduction

The previous chapters have examined key concepts which have focused on the effect of trauma on children and young people. Their experiences have left them overwhelmed with emotional pain and unbearable anxieties and emotions, which have become internalised. Consequently, they find the challenges they have to face when managing reality too stressful, putting them at real risk of breaking down psychologically, physically and emotionally. This prevents them from functioning – a situation which can result in their sense of self ceasing to evolve, remaining dormant and developmentally delayed. The next important theme to consider is the role of the practitioner who works directly with these young people. In today's world, what does this mean for those who are helping children and young people to recover from the traumatic experiences they have been subjected to throughout their lives?

Adler (1972:45) wrote that it was important to examine therapists' feelings of helplessness at times of change to mental health training and the modification of older treatment methods. His concern was that 'attractive new treatment modalities' promised rapid results which could at the same time turn attention away from the crucial task of therapists empathising with their patients and 'to be able to stand the discomforts of what they empathically hear, and to be able to use their affective responses to the patient as part of their evaluation of the patient and the way to proceed therapeutically'.

Although his paper was written in the early 1970s, the concerns are as relevant today as they were then. The 1970s and 1980s were periods of innovation, change and creative thinking. Since that time, things have continued to change, especially with the huge advancements in neuroscience. Legislation has addressed challenging issues, including child sexual abuse, trafficking, the anti-social tendency and violence; however, workers have not received appropriate support. They find themselves reacting to the hostility of difficult-to-manage children and young people, which often results in the escalation of aggressive behaviour. Yet despite the policy and practice guidelines that emerged from 2004 onwards, there are still a growing number of traumatised children and young people who are in need of greater specialist care to address the depth of their emotional damage. It is acknowledged that legislation that informs policy and practice is critical; however, it does not provide carers and other professionals with the knowledge and insight needed to address and meet the emotional needs of those for whom they are responsible.

It is important to understand that for many children and young people who have been traumatised throughout their life, the emotional pain has remained unrecognised by others. In order to survive, their thoughts and emotions remain buried in their inner world, unable to be thought about or worked through. Instead, they find a way of masking their panic and rage from others, in denial of their unbearable feelings. They present themselves as charming, only to break down when they experience the outside world as being there to attack and punish them, mirroring their early childhood experiences. This can lead them to act out their panic and rage, attacking back because they feel they are being persecuted by the outside world, often with dire consequences. The complexity of their difficulties is that because they have little or no sense of self-esteem they cannot accept personal responsibility for their actions; nor can they make reparation for the emotional and physical damage they have caused. As a consequence, they become locked into compulsively repeating destructive and traumatic experiences for themselves and others. Inevitably, this can make it very difficult for workers to deliver a therapeutic treatment programme leading to a good outcome for the child or young person. When the emotional life of the child for whom they are responsible is so painful and difficult to access, it makes the task of the worker quite onerous. To gain the necessary skills, insight and understanding necessary to help the child or young person feel emotionally contained and appropriately nurtured, workers require training and supervision. This is not an easy task, but crucial if there is to be a gain for both workers and children.

As I reflect on my years as a practitioner, trainer, consultant and psychotherapist across many social care and therapeutic environments, addressing policy and practice in relation to the concept of integration and unintegration, the most inspirational, yet at times most deeply painful, experiences that remain within me come from the Cotswold Community. What were the factors during my time there which made it a transformational place to work in? On reflection, the five key points are:

- a strong philosophical underpinning with a constant examination of our practice and values in the work with adolescents

- being helped to understand more about the delinquent acting out of adolescents and what their behaviours represented in terms of their early experiences of deprivation and trauma

- being taught to anticipate the adolescents' difficult behaviour rather than reacting to them, which only served to heighten their acting out

- understanding about the importance of 'shared experiences' between the staff team and the young people and developing insight into and understanding about the significance of a breakdown of communication and how this could create acting out in the adolescents

- the need for a clear organisational structure of the homes and the whole organisational structure to contain the complexities of delivering sound therapeutic practice.

At the Cotswold Community, a child breaking down or acting out anti-social or challenging behaviour was not simply left by the managers. The challenging behaviour was seen as being triggered by the breakdown of communication between the staff team and the adolescents. It was not only the young people who needed help and support to learn from their experience; it was the team also who needed an opportunity to reflect and to develop insight and understanding about their work practice.

■ CASE STUDY: BREAKDOWN OF COMMUNICATION BETWEEN WORKERS CREATING ACTING OUT IN THE CHILDREN AND YOUNG PEOPLE GROUP

In 1974, I was working as a therapeutic resource in one of the group living homes for eight adolescent boys at the Cotswold Community, most of whom had been assessed as functioning at the level of fragile emotional integration. There was one very troubled 14-year-old boy, Dave, who went home one weekend to visit his mother, from whom he was desperate to gain attention. On returning home, he found her in bed with a man he did not know, and she ignored him for most of the weekend. On his return to the Community he was full of anger and rage about what had occurred at home. His experience of communication breakdown between himself and his mother coincided with the difficulties the staff team were experiencing with the poor quality of communication between themselves; because they were not able to discuss their difficulties, it created a split in their relationships. This led to a chaotic dynamic in the home, and for Dave it reflected his difficult home situation. There was poor communication between the staff team themselves and the young people, and the panic and rage Dave carried increased and strengthened. During the evening Dave could not sleep and in the early hours of the following day he set fire to the building. It was found in time and, fortunately, apart from building damage, no one was injured.

The aftermath of this incident acted as a catalyst for change at the Community – culturally, professionally and psychologically – reframing the therapeutic work and practice with children and young people. Richard Balbernie, Principal of the Community, insisted that the staff team worked together until an understanding could be reached of what had created such an aggressive form of acting out by the young person. For two days, we were in constant discussion about the dynamics of the team and how our own breakdown of communication influenced and disrupted the culture of the adolescent group, converting it into a subculture, as our own group dynamics became more complex. The interpersonal denial of our own anxieties and uncertainties about each other and the young people had led to the culture of the group becoming non-functioning. After an exhausting and painful two days, we reached a deeper insight and understanding about the work and could identify the main ingredients needed for a successful therapeutic culture to evolve and be shared. A week later we opened up a new home for the young people to live in, which was named Springfield, where the staff team used the insight they had gained to implement the therapeutic practice guidelines. In time, the work and practice presented to the adolescents helped their outcomes to be more positive, as the therapeutic culture became richer and more meaningful to them.

For me, the most significant and profound learning from this experience was the staff team's ability to reflect and communicate with each other about the pain and anxiety that had emerged from the work in which they were involved. This quality of thinking deepened their awareness with insight and understanding about their relationships with the children and young people for whom they were responsible. During my ten years at the Cotswold Community, the experience was at times extremely painful yet also deeply inspirational, becoming more so when I began to see the results in the emotional development of the young people. Since that time, although the Cotswold Community is no longer in operation, the learning lies in the legacy that I have been able to carry with me. I have retained what I learned from working at the Community, developing the concept of integration and unintegration and weaving it into current thinking and practice. It is not only a matter of understanding the key concepts, but also, importantly, involves supporting workers to be able to withstand the pain of putting it into practice.

The primary task meets the impossible task

The primary task in our work is to meet the emotional needs of traumatised children, and it can be likened to building the foundation on which a house can be built for the child to live in, with comfort and security. Once it is established, the secondary task is to furnish a variety of rooms where different aspects of living can take place. This can be likened to the child who is developing a sense of self where the rooms represent varying aspects of their personality, some of which enable them to function, and others which mean they still remain vulnerable and find stress difficult to manage. The issue when working with traumatised and emotionally vulnerable children and young people is that they lack the basis for healthy emotional development. Balbernie (1971) highlighted the need to both define the starting point and identify the basic principles of the work to be carried out, which comprised:

1. defining the primary task and the significance of task confusion and its effect on staff

2. ensuring continuous accurate assessment

3. maintaining a clear baseline: to establish what the issues are for the whole group, what structure is suitable for each individual and what a satisfactory outcome would look like.

What Balbernie outlined was that, for child care workers to survive, they had to know a) what was damaged, and (b) what the treatment should be. The workers could then identify the appropriateness of provision and treatment. When workers are treating unintegrated children and young people, the primary task is to identify and meet the children's emotional needs, helping them feel emotionally contained and held in the mind of their carers enough that their self begins to strengthen and grow.

The secondary task provides the ingredients to make it work successfully. These can vary from organisation to organisation, depending on the main focus of their working environment.

To outline the formulation of the primary task to the workers is important, but helping them to fulfil the task successfully is another matter. The child or young person's sense of hopelessness and helplessness is projected and transferred on to the worker. Without appropriate support and supervision, it can make the task quite unbearable at times. It is important that they are taught the concept of transference and counter-transference in a therapeutic environment. David Wills wrote:

> If you have a boundless and invincible faith in what you are doing, and that faith is based in the unchanging and eternal verities, you will survive. But if your confidence in what you do is based on some pragmatic assessment of its value, measured against the yardstick of some human scientific concept, then I advise you to keep bees or become a business tycoon. (1971a:342)

Wills's belief was that if we are to face the overwhelming sense of hopelessness, anxiety and uncertainty in the world of traumatised children and young people, we must not allow ourselves to build a sense of denial about their emotional hurt and pain. This plasters over an increasing gap between their inner-world experiences that make life unbearable for them and the external world of reality, which becomes more complex and difficult to reach out to when they need to face the challenges of life. Plasters can easily fall off the skin, leaving the hurt to continue bleeding and not heal. Workers need to reach an awareness of the internal working model of the young person, holding on to the hurt and emotional pain they carry with them.

The theory of the impossible task is the basic assumption among workers and professionals that those they are responsible for cannot change except in a superficial way (Dockar-Drysdale 1973). There is considerable evidence in current practice to substantiate the view that although children and young people may present themselves as changing, this change is experienced by some professionals as being superficial, even if it is described and accepted by some institutions and managing bodies as representing a good outcome. It is important to recognise that superficial change can mask panic and rage. These emotions locked inside the child's inner world can be acted out violently and aggressively, occasioned by any stress factor and with serious consequences. The outcome of this behaviour can be a return to institutional care, leading to an increase of recidivism in the prison and young offenders sector. As practitioners and consultants we can all feel helpless and hopeless when we are faced with the depth of unbearable emotions that have remained in the inner world of those we are responsible for. When they do eventually emerge, they are too powerful for the young person to manage and they transfer the emotions on to their workers. Without useful supervision and consultation, workers find it difficult not to react when it touches the emotionally vulnerable aspects of themselves. But as the magnitude of the task increases, so do the doubts and uncertainties of the worker and with this their anxiety about the work. Without access to supervised support and an opportunity for reflection when faced with the projection of primitive anxieties and emotions and where the child is neither willing nor able to demonstrate a sense of responsibility, the primary task becomes impossible to achieve.

So how do we find the way forwards in our work practice, delivering a treatment plan to the child or young person that can help them progress towards a successful outcome during their stay with us? Workers need to be able to help them to promote their belief in themselves as an individual with a sense of self which they value such that they can look towards their future development with a desire to fulfil their expectations. When under stress, the child needs to allow their emotional responses to occur without negatively affecting others, having developed the capacity to think about their actions and accept personal responsibility. We need to accept that the primary task must be based on developing the child's capacity, in Winnicott's terms, 'to be', and the secondary task must support the child and young person in functioning and managing the realities and challenges in the outside world.

The way forward, making it work

1 Assessing emotional needs

Workers should be able to identify and assess children's emotional needs, giving them a greater clarity about the impact of traumatic experiences on their developing sense of self. Children need help to recognise the elements of provision and support they need if they are to reach a level of emotional integration, starting to recover from the emotional pain of their traumas, through the use of a treatment programme.

2 The facilitating environment

To support the use of a treatment programme in a therapeutic setting, the environmental factors play a key role. The facilitating environment does not make children develop emotionally, but it can provide enough physical structure and sense of safety to enable them to use the care and treatment being offered to them. Winnicott (1990:223) wrote, 'The environment does not make the infant grow, nor does it determine the direction of growth. The environment when good enough can provide for and facilitate the maturational process.' A considerable level of dependence on the worker is essential for the unintegrated child or young person to reach the stage of being able to make a significant attachment relationship. It is the environment which is the initial 'place to be', giving them a strong message about what their stay in the placement will offer them. The facilitating environment should provide a child-centred culture of physical safety, predictability and reliability, in which they feel held in the mind of those who are responsible for them.

3 Culture and subculture

The way of living and being in a therapeutic environment is crucial for treatment and practice to be successful. A team of workers should always discuss the quality of culture in their environment and what it offers to the children or young people. A subculture where the practice, values and beliefs diverge from the cultural values in the environment can be detrimental to the functioning of the whole group. It can be quite destructive to the delivery of good therapeutic practice, and can turn the implementation of the primary task over to a culture of anti-task, preventing good therapeutic practice from developing.

4 Reflective practice

Workers require the space and opportunity to be engaged in reflective discussion about their work and the impact on them of some of the unbearable feelings in the young people.

5 Key concepts

Workers need to address the following key concepts, in their ongoing work with the children and young people:

- transference and counter-transference (see the glossary)

- projective identification (see the glossary)

- fantasy and reality factors in therapeutic work

- communication at a verbal, symbolic and non-verbal level.

Conclusion

This chapter has highlighted the importance of practitioners recognising, thinking about and understanding the world of traumatised children. Understanding this world will inspire us to continue delivering the practice and treatment methods which the book describes. We need to believe that this understanding can continuously move forwards to integrate with current thinking and practice. What comes to my mind is a conversation which took place shortly after the experience of the Cotswold Community fire and its aftermath. I was working in the new Springfield home one day, still feeling quite depressed after what had happened. I was visited by the then Head of Education, Michael Jinks, who said to me, 'I wanted to come and tell you that if you can believe the new primary task you are embarking on will work and come through the darkness you find yourself in, then it will work, and the light will be seen again. But if you begin to think that it cannot, then it will stop and previous difficulties will be re-enacted. So do carry on believing that the new task can move forward with you.'

It was a truly helpful statement and gave me the belief that the new task could develop and grow, helping the young people to become stronger in themselves. I have continued to develop this way of thinking about the inner world of traumatised children, enabling it to improve outcomes for young people. If taking a task forward and making it work is based on a fundamental belief that it will work, then it can pull through and develop. If workers and practitioners can go through the darkness and unbearable aspects of their work, at times feeling overwhelmed by their own anxieties and uncertainties, they will be able to help the children and young people they are responsible for to manage their own darkness and fears, and to see their future in a brighter light.

PART 2

APPLYING THE CONCEPTS IN DIFFERENT SETTINGS

CHAPTER 7

HOW IT WORKS

Christine Bradley

We live in a multi-cultural society in which there is diversity in the way child development is seen and understood. Working with children and young people who have been deeply traumatised by their childhood experiences has been considered by many. In this ever-changing landscape, it is important that basic assumptions about the nature of this work can be challenged, with differing concepts about its practice becoming culturally and philosophically integrated and thought about contextually. The important point to consider is whether the concepts discussed within the preceding chapters are valid and transferable to other contexts and settings. Certain concepts can be influenced by the expectations of others, culturally and conceptually. According to Music:

> It is argued that attachment theory is a universal biological system and yet like all other theories it developed within a particular time and with a specific cultural framework. While the nuances of attachment relationships might differ across cultures, and some attachment concepts might have some cultural bias, overall attachment theory appears to have a significant applicability across cultures. (2011:68)

Clearly the work of John Bowlby and Donald Winnicott has been key in the conceptual and theoretical thinking of the 20th century.

In 1958 Bruno Bettelheim, as the Director of the Orthogenic School in Chicago and reporting on work with disturbed children and identifying the difficulties of helping them which were encountered in his work, wrote:

The deviation in personality development shown by these children allows for important conclusions. It demonstrates the danger of child rearing in a setting where a number of adults take care of the isolated functions of the child rather than the whole child, and stresses the necessity of giving each child the opportunity for a continuous central relationship with one adult in the institution. (1948:106)

Bettelheim used his determination and pioneering spirit to work towards changing the lives of traumatised children. This came from his own personal traumas through the experience of surviving Dachau and Buchenwald concentration camps during the Second World War. It had left him with a deep passion and determination to challenge and tackle the inhumanity of mental institutions. The foundation of the Orthogenic School in Chicago resulted from this drive and compassion.

Where does the pioneering work tackled with such compassion, research and thinking about the emotional world of the child throughout the 20th century leave us today? There is a far greater awareness and insight of the effect of early deprivation and neglect on children globally. The knowledge base of workers, carers and professionals is higher and more focused than at an earlier date, and this enables them to tackle their difficulties more effectively. Although the reality factors of different cultures vary, and certain viewpoints can be biased against each other, what is acknowledged and generally agreed is that the quality of the maternal and infantile relationship is crucial for the emotional well-being of the developing child. We are currently reaching out to children and young people whose cultures have been destroyed and they have had to flee their war-torn countries. Many have lost parents and are in powerful and overwhelmingly traumatic, emotional states. How they deal with and manage their trauma will be influenced by:

- the part of the world they have fled to, and the culture of their new country in accepting and providing for them physically, practically and personally

- the quality of their early primary relationship, which determines their level of emotional integration. They may be holding on to feelings of trust and safety, having internalised a secure base because of the emotional richness and strength they took from their primary attachment and relationship with their carer (emotional integration). Or, they may remain unintegrated, because they did not feel held in the mind of their primary carer. To survive they became a law unto themselves, unable to share the world with others or manage the challenges of external reality (unintegration).

The integrated child will struggle with a tragic and painful sense of loss from a relationship that was secure and meaningful for them with their primary carer. They require a great amount of support and help to manage their depressive anxieties, and to re-establish themselves in their new environment.

In contrast, the unintegrated child prior to being forced into refugee status felt emotionally and physically abandoned by their primary carer. Because this left them with feelings of anger, sadness and rage in their inner world, it could leave them in danger of becoming over-identified with war-torn areas in the external world, as their early experiences of emotional abandonment left them feeling at war between themselves and others. These children and young people are more likely to require specialist care and therapeutic treatment if they are to re-establish themselves in their new setting without acting out destructively through violent and aggressive behaviour.

With every theoretical concept which develops, there is always a starting point where a foundation stone is laid, leaving room for the practitioners to use it as the concept grows and develops. The work of Bowlby, Winnicott and Bettelheim illustrates that it is through their knowledge and insight developed through their own belief, determination and compassion which helps their theories to formulate as a concept for others, when helping traumatised children and young people.

Although discussed earlier, I want to bring in the work of Dockar-Drysdale who, with the support of Winnicott, laid the foundation stone for the concept of integration and unintegration as a starting point for good therapeutic practice. The concept became embedded in therapeutic work and practice at the Mulberry Bush School during the 1960s and 1970s, where she continued to evolve a programme for assessing the emotional needs of the children who were placed there. She also took the step of integrating the concept into the work of the Cotswold Community, where she was therapeutic consultant until 1994. The low levels of breakdown in both the Mulberry Bush School and the Cotswold Community show the impact of her work. A very high percentage of young people reached a stage of emotional recovery and made a successful transition to the next stage of their life, either through fostering or returning home.

Over the past 15 years, the work has been used to align the concept with the conceptual frameworks being used in research and practice today, aiming to achieve good and successful outcomes for children and young people. If the concept is to continue helping them to develop a sense of living and being with which they feel more comfortable, then we need to continue moving the concept forwards in our work practice. However, for workers to be successful with this way of working, there are a number of obstacles to be tackled and hurdles to be cleared. The evidence so far tells us that it is possible to achieve success for traumatised children and young people.

The following chapters will discuss and portray how the concepts examined earlier can be applied in different settings:

- residential care

- leading a therapeutic community

- fostering and post-adoption

- the unintegrated adolescent.

CHAPTER 8

THERAPEUTIC CARE AND TREATMENT OF CHILDREN AND YOUNG PEOPLE IN RESIDENTIAL CARE

Christine Bradley

Introduction

The enormity and complexity of the professional task in residential child care has not been valued and recognised as much as it deserves. It can be an overwhelming experience for workers to encounter the underlying fears and uncertainties that are buried in the inner lives of children and young people they are responsible for in residential care. There is an ever-increasing demand on carers and professionals to achieve a good outcome for children and young people who are in need of specialist care and provision, and to produce the evidence required to support their results. But what does this mean for those workers?

Children and young people who live with the traumatic experiences they were subjected to in their early years require specialist care and treatment to enable them to begin to recover from their trauma and to reach a stage where they can maintain the balance between managing the demands of the outside world (reality) and fulfilling their own emotional needs. It can make the primary task workers are required to follow complex, difficult and at times stressful. However, it is also important they recognise that, with appropriate support, supervision and a sound knowledge base provided in the workplace, it is perfectly possible to achieve a good outcome for the child or young person. There is an increase in the number of unintegrated children who break down; many cannot manage the foster home placements because they find the intimacy of personal relationships unbearable, and respond by trying to destroy them. A small group-care setting could be more appropriate in the first instance, providing the opportunity for them to reach an emotional starting point from which attachment and fostering could begin. This can make the residential task difficult for workers to hold on to. Anglin and Miller (n.d.) stated:

> All the young people in residential care, and most of those in the child welfare system, have experienced many losses, traumas and disappointments, and live with deep psycho-emotional pain. We need to avoid inflicting more pain on their pain, and to help them to gain a sense of becoming shapers of their own destinies, rather than feeling like victims of fate.

What does this mean for workers who are aiming to meet the emotional needs of unintegrated children who have little or no sense of self? Because these children have been so preoccupied with surviving their difficult times, they have not yet been able to build up healthy defence mechanisms to protect themselves from difficult or painful circumstances in their life. It is difficult for workers to manage their personal and professional lives while dealing with the complexity of the work needed to support the emotional lives of the children and young people with whom they work. A change in the dynamic of the staff team and how it is managed can influence the culture and dynamic of the child and young person's group.

The two case studies that follow are examples of workers' responses to children with whom they have worked with, showing how to respond appropriately to the child at their most painful time and when they overreact, leaving the child with a profound sense of chaos and a feeling of being under attack.

■ CASE STUDY: HOLLY

The manager of a children's home I was doing some consulting with was leaving to take up a more senior role in the organisation. Although the move was managed well by himself and the team of workers, I informed them that, for the adolescents who were placed in the home, it could bring up a number of primitive feelings about being abandoned by people on whom they were dependent. Although the reality factor for the team as to why the manager was leaving and separating from his role in the home was practically and professionally well managed, for the inner reality of the young people it remained unthinkable and unbearable to take in for a period until it was worked through and understood with help and support from their workers.

During my meeting with the staff team a few weeks after the manager had left, we were discussing the impact on the group living experience for the staff team. A female worker said to me, 'The other evening when I had been working with Holly, I panicked because she was saying such horrible things to me and made me feel awful. I have never felt like that before, I did get over it, but it was awful.' I explained to the worker that Holly was projecting all her own unbearable feelings of anger and rage about losing people who had a meaning for her; the manager leaving had perhaps left her feeling let down by the rest of the staff team, which led her to act out aggressively towards them. Because Holly's worker took in some of her primitive emotions and behaviour without reacting back, it did help her to continue functioning, although it left her worker feeling terrible for a period of time.

A male worker then described feeling overwhelmed by the young people when they disrupted their own group dynamics one evening by 'merging' as a pair and planning to act out destructively. He wondered if he wanted to continue working there, although he did soon work through and recover from such feelings. This was the first time he had felt so deeply attacked by the emotions of the young people, and he found it a very powerful experience, which he wanted to think about.

Finding their own psychic space, where they could communicate about some of their own unbearable feelings they experience in their work, helped these two workers to gain insight and understanding about the dynamics of the young person's group and how they affected them. It helped to prevent them from reacting back to the young person. When children are also experiencing unconscious pressures from each other, transference and projective identification are ubiquitous.

At the time, Holly had been placed in the home for two years and two emotional need assessment programmes had been written for her. She had been assessed as functioning at the level of unintegration within the syndrome of an archipelago child; she also held levels of functioning which could break down under stress. Holly had a very low sense of self with little or no self-esteem, and at times of stress she could become suicidal and self-harming. The team had been implementing her treatment programme over the following months. As a result, her level of ego integration and sense of self had begun to strengthen. However, at times of stress she could disintegrate and experience the outside world as attacking her, and this could lead her to retreat back to suicidal tendencies. The workers came to realise that Holly believed the departure of the home's manager had taken place because she was so disliked by him and horrible and he no longer wanted to be with her. They helped her to realise that this was her own fantasy, because she felt so awful about herself sometimes, and not the reality as to why he had moved on in his work. When we are working with unintegrated children or young people, it is so easy for the two realities between the child and the worker at times of stress to remain split off from each other. This can bring about serious acting out if it is not responded to by the worker.

CASE STUDY: RONNIE

Ronnie had been placed in a children's home for one year. The day I visited there was a high level of concern about his placement, because he had acted out violently to one of his female workers and broken her nose. The workers wondered if they would be able to contain him. Ronnie had been traumatised physically and sexually abused as a child, and although he was an adolescent, he presented as a small child. Ronnie carried a high amount of panic and rage in his inner world, which he acted out, resulting in breaking the nose of the worker. However, he continued to present himself as a quiet and lost child, who found it difficult to communicate through words.

I met with Ronnie and explained to him that I needed to understand what led him to become so overwhelmed with angry feelings that he attacked one of the workers in the home. Was it because he felt they were going to attack him? He began to tell me that because his parents used to beat him and lock him up if he was naughty, he was afraid the same was going to happen in the home. During that time Ronnie spoke to me with such deep pain and sadness in him it touched me. While driving home that evening I found myself crying, being so in touch with the panic and fear he had lived with throughout his childhood.

On my return the following month, I was informed by his workers that he had not had a violent episode since my last visit but he was still not able to verbally communicate with them or the child group. Ronnie wanted to speak to me again. I explained that after we had last spoken I felt very sad, and that perhaps that was because he was very sad also, which I was aware of. He began to cry and said that he had been sad all his life, but could never talk about it and did not know why. My consultation with the workers helped them to respond to his pain and sadness more than previously; consequently Ronnie became very settled in the home, as the workers were more in touch with his emotional needs and an assessment had identified him as a frozen child. They provided him with the primary experiences he required to 'unfreeze' his emotional life, with Ronnie beginning to learn from his behaviour and ask questions of others. In time, with the care and treatment he received from the home, Ronnie became more emotionally integrated, with a developing sense of self he believed in.

> Children who have suffered trauma in their earliest years and who have endured many further years of being misunderstood and let down will not readily allow themselves to be helped. Allowing trust to develop is very threatening. These children are likely to attack the effort of those trying to help them. (Tomlinson 2004:17)

The two case studies describe what it is like for workers to undertake appropriate care and treatment for these children and young people. They highlight how difficult it can be for the workers to live alongside the most painful and unbearable aspects of the children's inner world. We need to think about what is needed to create a therapeutic environment in residential care where those living in the home can begin to recover from their earlier traumatic experiences and start to view the outside world as a safe place to be, finding their part in it with a sense of trust.

Assessment of need

There is a growing recognition that an attachment cycle cannot appropriately apply to all young people and that a profile of avoidant attachment can be an outward sign of inner unintegration. The inner world of the child or young person has to be the starting point and main focus of the work. It is all too easy for difficult-to-manage behaviour to be labelled with an attachment disorder diagnosis, when the child has not yet reached the starting point for emotional growth to develop through attachment relationships.

Emotional need assessment programmes can prevent workers and carers from making assumptions about difficult-to-manage behaviour without an understanding about what the behaviour represents in terms of the child's inner-world experiences of trauma and abuse. Such insight from the worker could prevent a placement from breaking down, if the worker can reach a deeper understanding about the child's behaviour, and how they can respond appropriately to the child. The treatment programme provides the tools with which therapeutic practice can develop between the worker and the child or young person.

The facilitating environment

The term 'facilitating environment' was coined by Winnicott and refers to the context or environment a 'good enough mother' is able to create for her baby in which to live and grow. In residential care, the facilitating environment means a highly structured and contained setting where the unmet emotional needs of children and young people at an early stage of their development can be recognised, understood and provided for. The key component of the concept is that of 'leadership', which determines an approach towards the work and is organisational and creative in attitude towards the staff team. This leads workers to be as conducive as possible to maintaining a positive attitude and contributing to a good outcome that can be maintained by the children and young people. Leadership that develops and nurtures a facilitating environment in the children's home allows room for emotional and physical containment for the children, while leaving the space for creative thinking about the work and practice with them. It could facilitate workers' best work in the therapeutic care and treatment of the young people for whom they are responsible.

Support, supervision and consultation for workers

If residential workers are to fulfil the therapeutic task positively, with a strong element of success for those they are responsible for, the question often asked is: How can the workers develop insight and understanding about the dynamics of the young person's behaviour?

The response to this is that, by increasing their ability to reflect, think and develop, workers will realise that the insight needed to help them understand the behaviour is not always about what is happening on the surface of the child's behaviour, but more about the child's inner world (Bradley 2010).

If workers can think, understand and develop some insight into what at times feels to be their own unbearable feelings, the more possible it is for them to be able to help and support the children or young people to understand and live through theirs. The following guidance is needed to support workers with their personal and professional development:

- Reflective practice. At the end of each day the staff team should come together to discuss how they are feeling, having been with the children and young people. Their own negative or positive emotions about the day will give them an understanding of the emotional life of the young people at that time of the day, with some insight into their awareness and responses to them on the following day.

- If workers are left feeling vulnerable or anxious, this could be a sign that the young person is experiencing similar emotions but is not able to think about them.

- Workers need supervision, individually and with the team of other workers as a group supervision.

- Appropriate training is needed, introducing them to the concept of integration and unintegration.

Conclusion

When working and living alongside the emotional vulnerability and rawness of children and young people who require the care and treatment approach of residential care, it should be recognised that the worker plays a central role. Workers who can remain in touch with the inner world of the child or young person may find the experience very difficult and at times painful as the work brings up personal feelings of hopelessness and helplessness. If therapeutic practice is to develop and grow in the field of residential care and treatment, it is important that workers are provided with the support and consultation needed to help them develop a deeper understanding about some of the more unbearable aspects of the work. There are times in the life of a residential worker when they wonder why they are doing this work, but there are also other times when they see a child or young person, after a period of aggressive acting out towards a worker, wanting to make reparation for their behaviour and accepting personal responsibility for their actions. This is what I have described as the wow factor, when one sees true change and maturation in a child or young person.

Winnicott (1970), when presenting the David Wills lecture, observed:

> Residential care is a combination of loving, hating and surviving. There has to be a belief in workers that disaster can be repaired and rebuilt and failure can be healed.

Finding a new starting point in their life from which to develop signals the point from which the child begins to function as a person in their own right as an individual. As they develop emotionally, they can start to think about their emotions before they break down and act out. The provision of care and treatment can be a very important factor, when the sense of self feels more real and meaningful to them as they start to experience the outside world as being potentially more manageable and bearable. Residential care for children and young people can be a huge asset when professionals try to find ways of helping them with their emotional difficulties, and it should be recognised as such. It is imperative that all workers receive the appropriate training, support and supervision needed if they are to develop the skills required to understand children's behaviour and respond accordingly.

CHAPTER 9

LEADING AND MANAGING A THERAPEUTIC COMMUNITY

John Diamond

Introduction

Early in my career, I became a household manager at the Cotswold Community. I was responsible for a staff team and a group of up to ten severely emotionally troubled adolescent boys.

For many years, the concepts of leadership and management were at the periphery of my thinking. I saw leadership and management as 'attributes' that other people, mainly in business or the armed forces, needed in relation to their ability to run companies or to maintain the ability to command when 'thinking under fire'. I think the combination of attributes and skills that enable people to lead and manage within residential care settings are complex, and they are not necessarily easily defined by the expectations sought in our current 'managerialist' culture.

At that time, being a manager or 'in management' was not an expression I used. I focused more on a sort of ground-level intuition of 'getting on with my job', and trying to do this to the best of my ability. But I knew intuitively and instinctively, and through the necessity of having at times to 'survive' challenging situations, that good role modelling and 'open communication' were the best ways of getting a team to work together. The collective struggle to create clear boundaries and caring, respectful relationships was the foundation for finding a way of living together.

With time, my work became guided and grounded through psychodynamic thinking. The basic tenet for therapeutic management was along the lines of, 'If we get the relationships and the "facilitating environment" right, then the traumatised young people in our care will be given the optimum conditions for positive social and emotional growth.'

Leadership is sometimes said to require followership. I disagree with this. I am accountable to those in senior positions to me, but I do not feel that I follow anyone, nor do I ever expect anyone to follow me. However, I do expect people to do their job as best they can. I do not think job satisfaction and good morale are created by people being 'told what to do'. I think they are created by the coalescence of good internal and external experiences – the 'fit' between the values of the person/ality and those of the working environment, and identification with a meaningful task.

Textbooks tend to generalise to say that leadership implies vision and strategy, and management implies 'operationalising' the vision and strategy. I think this is simplistic and too linear a concept – real life and the use of both imaginative vision and of personal and institutional authority are much more complex, fluid and dynamic processes.

Role and function

Often within residential child care, and especially children's homes, the 'registered manager' has to act as, and integrate, both the roles of leader and manager. As a leader, they will be responsible for the future strategic development of the home, but will also have to manage the staff team. Through the enactment of their managerial function *with* the staff team, collectively the manager and staff are responsible for the provision of a caring and nurturing environment, and the safety and welfare of the child group.

At the Mulberry Bush School, we have separated out some of the 'functions' of leadership and management, which people now hold at different distances or 'boundaries' in relation to the core or 'primary' task. Understanding 'the primary task' is important, as I shall explore in the next section. The primary task is defined here as 'the task the enterprise must perform in order to survive', or, as it is currently defined by Ofsted, the home's 'statement of purpose'.

The Mulberry Bush School and the primary task

The Mulberry Bush School is a residential school and therapeutic community providing specialist integrated therapeutic care, treatment and education to traumatised children aged 5–13 and their families. Due to extreme anxiety-inducing behaviours, stemming from severe social, emotional, mental health and complex needs, the children are referred by local authorities from across the UK. Our aim is to reintegrate children back into an appropriate family, school and local community.

As a result of early years and complex trauma, the children struggle to make meaningful relationships and develop a sense of belonging to their birth or substitute families. Without an early intervention, their mistrustful, aggressive, chaotic and confused behaviours will be re-enacted in later life. Our work aims to strengthen the child's relationship with their family and society, to break abusive cycles and reduce the future risk of offending.

Staff work together in multi-disciplinary 'treatment teams' to ensure each child's social, emotional and educational needs are met across each three-year placement.

The primary task

Within residential care generally it is the responsibility of leaders and managers to keep this concept of 'primary task or purpose' as a central tenet or principle that underpins all of the work. It defines which children and young people the home or school will work with, their age range and whether they have social, emotional and mental health difficulties, autism spectrum disorders or other special educational needs and disabilities. At the Mulberry Bush School, we see our primary task as 'the care, treatment and education of severely emotionally troubled children aged 5–13 and their families'.

However, although this might be the primary task of the school, in my current role as Chief Executive Officer (CEO), I have to keep this in mind in relation to my more direct responsibility to ensure delivery of the broader charitable mission of the Mulberry Bush Organisation, which is 'to reach more children and their families'.

Within organisations we have to make use of both our personal authority and institutional authority to maintain an ongoing alignment with delivery of the primary task. Institutional authority is the authority invested in someone in their role by the organisation. There is always a dynamic interplay between the person and their role, and therefore how personal authority is enacted within an institutional role.

Strategy as a collective task

From our experience, we have come to regard the development of our strategy or 'strategic evolution' as a dynamic process that emerges out of continuously evolving interactions. This suggests that no one person owns, holds or creates the strategy. It has developed out of a constant flow of interconnected ideas from individuals and teams within the organisation, and from outside the organisation by the daily influence of the 'material' – facts, assumptions and thoughts that are picked up via discussions, news and national or regional policy formation, and needs that are identified through new working relationships.

This information or 'material' is made up of a myriad of ideas, some fully formed and some evolving. As such, strategic vision can modify on a daily basis with the internalisation of each new piece of information. Ideas and information constantly cross the boundary of the organisation, and the boundaries of the subsystems. There is a constantly shifting 'organisation in the mind' of each member of staff (and children). This leads us to the question: Where is strategy? The answer is: It is in everyone's heads.

In this sense, if leaders or managers can 'tap into' the interests and vision of staff, they are more likely to find that there are many aspects of people's collective (and often unspoken) thinking that can help identify and clarify 'what binds them together'. Ultimately, by finding ways of tapping into this unseen resource, and making it conscious, we can develop a shared understanding of how the strategy is thought about and developed. This process can also help create bridges between professional disciplines and acts like a 'glue' that adheres people in service to the common (primary) task.

Creating a system where each person is 'their own manager'

We have worked hard over the years to delegate responsibility and trust downwards to front-line workers. We have consciously attempted to empower staff who work directly with the children to form caring and safe relationships, to create a culture where they can 'be their own managers', i.e. take responsibility for their work, and be accountable to their team colleagues as the primary reference point for this work. At the Mulberry Bush School, the residential and education teams develop their own working cultures and take collective responsibility for the delivery of each programme of therapeutic care and education.

Staff are still ultimately accountable to their line manager for this work, but the emphasis is on the staff member to take responsibility for their direct work, and the role of managers is to support and monitor the quality of this work. We also expect all staff to be accountable and share their learning experiences with their household, class and treatment team colleagues. The aim is to create an ongoing learning culture or 'culture of enquiry' through the use of support structures such as group supervision and our 'reflective spaces'.

We work on the embedded cultural belief that if we offer trust and give our front-line staff real responsibility and accountability, everyone in the organisation will be empowered to feel like an adult, and will give their best accordingly.

Themes

Theme 1: Management at the boundary

This is largely the theme of this chapter and presents an exploration of how the concept of 'management at the boundary' allows leaders and managers to inhabit and sustain the 'Janus' position. The Janus position is named after the Roman god who was positioned at the wall of the city and had two faces: one facing inwards and one outwards.

The Janus position implies the ability of staff to look both internally 'inside' their area of responsibility within the organisation's boundary, to ensure the appropriate delivery of the service, and externally, at the dynamics and processes that influence parts of the workplace.

At times, people and the boundaries they inhabit are enacted, or felt as rigid or 'impermeable', but at other times, they are experienced as more elastic or permeable. Sometimes when there are high levels of acting out and the school feels 'uncontained' there is a need for the people at these boundaries around the child to act as shock absorbers, and the boundaries become more rigid and firm. At these times, a benign form of the 'command and control' structure is used to re-establish safety and order. At other times when the community is more 'contained' – calm and settled – these boundaries are less visible, and more elastic or 'permeable'. This is why effective delegation is essential, and especially delegation to people who can really manage their area of task responsibility.

The boundary position strategically enables the one 'in charge' at each specific moment – whether they are a care worker with a responsibility for shift co-ordination, a teacher managing a classroom or a senior manager – to regulate and make links and connections between the inner and outer worlds of their task area.

I see the function or 'position' of my role as CEO as remaining at the boundary of the charity as an organisation. This boundary position has a number of qualities: it enables me to 'look inwards' to be supportive of colleagues and, through good communication from colleagues, maintain some understanding of the 'emotional temperature' of each day. It also fulfils something of the role of organisational 'gatekeeper' to the overall task, implying the function of a 'filter' or 'shock absorber' to issues that reach the boundary from either inside or outside of the organisation. I also work very much across the boundary, 'out into the societal environment', to ensure that the school has a good profile and sector reputation and is growing its sphere of influence. I do this through marketing, advertising and promoting our work at conferences and trade fairs. My aim is to engage with as many relevant external agencies as possible.

As CEO, I also feel it is important to role-model the 'way of being' and working in the community, and reflect that in my external work. I see these core attributes or skills as:

- developing trusting relationships

- working as a reflective practitioner.

When I am working on the school site, I do not cross my boundary to interfere in other people's areas of work, but I might comment or share my observations of their work, or ask someone to follow up an issue if I am unclear or concerned about a piece of work.

Reflective practice implies the ability to be prepared to think about one's actions in relation to the broader group, team and organisational context. It implies being prepared and able to see oneself more objectively, developing an internal 'third position' or 'consultancy stance'. To attempt to be able to reflect on one's actions, and oneself in action.

In relation to a reflective stance, staying at, or the ability to be able to return to, the boundary position creates an appropriate distance between thought and action, and enables each person to hold their area of responsibility in mind. A rule of thumb would be: 'If you cannot return to the boundary of your task area for which you have responsibility, have you become enmeshed in someone else's work?'

The management structure: the senior leadership team

At the Mulberry Bush School, the senior leadership team is called the 'Conducting Management Group' (CMG), comprising the director and the heads of the three main therapeutic task areas or 'departments': residential care or 'group living'; education; and therapies and networks team (therapists and family network practitioners). The group also includes a head of referrals and partnerships, a senior administrator and, finally, the head of our 'MBOX teaching school', which is our training and outreach department.

The conductor of an orchestra directs the component players and their instruments in order to play the symphony. At the Mulberry Bush School, the director is ultimately responsible for ensuring that the whole system is working harmoniously. The role of the director is to ensure integrated working across the areas, and each of these managers has responsibility for the delivery of high-quality therapeutic work and for developing their task area.

The other department managers are leaders of their task areas, and have to attempt to both understand and be in touch with each of the component parts of their task area. Their leadership ensures that there is both clarity and authority within each of the component subgroups. By working closely together, we create the full range of the 'lived experience' of provision that feels coherent and meaningful to the child group as a safe and nurturing experience. This is why the CMG is such an important forum for sharing perspectives and maintaining an integrated service.

Through their oversight, members of the CMG provide direction for the task, and a continuity of thinking for the organisation. Each component part of the task has someone ultimately 'in charge' and ensures that there is a sound oversight and accountability for each area.

Regular meetings ensure that each area is linked, and offer the ability to discuss and re-establish clarity if there is any confusion across boundaries. The CMG also works together to provide support to each other, and act as a 'think tank' if a member requires help in working through a specific issue.

The role of the director is to manage the interface between these task areas, and to ensure the quality of the overall provision. Open and direct communication is essential and, due to the demands of the task, the CMG attends its own 'reflective space' to untangle and clarify inevitable complications. The space occupied by the CMG defines the 'horizontal' structure to which the director belongs. As CEO, I use the CMG as my internal frame of reference, the board of trustees externally.

In this next section, I have identified the key tasks that we use to understand and effectively manage the therapeutic task of the Mulberry Bush School.

The key tasks of management and leadership in a therapeutic community environment

CREATING 'TRAUMA-INFORMED PRACTICE' –
UNDERSTANDING AND MANAGING PROJECTIONS

Because we are working with children who have experienced early years and complex trauma, we need to be a 'trauma-informed organisation' using trauma-informed practice. I would argue that an understanding of the psychoanalytic concepts of 'projective identification' (how strong feelings are 'put into' others, in order to get them to 'act out' that feeling) and the 'diagnostic' aspect of 'counter-transference' (what the feeling 'put into me' is, telling me about the state of mind of the other person) as real and dynamically active personal and group unconscious processes are the essential tools for understanding trauma-informed reflective practice.

Throughout their daily work, managers will have to manage an array of unwanted feelings that will be projected onto and into them. These feelings will include both the discontent of staff, often influenced by the strong feelings of the children. Daily, the staff groups will also contain undigested and raw experiences of strong feelings and anxiety projected into them by the children they work with. When working closely with children, staff will receive these conscious and unconscious communications (for example, they may feel that children are sometimes 'getting under their skin') as part of their work of managing challenging behaviours.

In this sense, as part of the treatment process it is useful to think of 'staff as the transference object' (Hinshelwood 1987) for the children. Adult staff members are consequently hated, loved, belittled, idealised and denigrated in the course of building relationships with the children. This work is, of course, essential if children are to work through their early experiences. For a further exploration of this process see the paper 'The Use of an Object and Relating through Identifications' (Winnicott 1968).

The task of the manager at these times is to be able to use the distance created by their boundary position, and the diagnostic aspects of counter-transference, to explore the nature of the projection. How does it make me feel? What am I being asked to do? Does the feeling associated link to direct work with situations in or across the boundary?

CREATING A 'PSYCHOLOGICAL PRESENCE'

Following the basic premise that the 'health' of the organisation reflects the health of the leadership, there is clearly a responsibility on management and leadership to promote a therapeutic environment with a containing, nurturing and purposeful ethos. The concept of 'all work being in service to the primary task' is a useful benchmark here.

If the leadership is psychologically absent, the boundary of the school as a system can feel to staff and children to be weakened. A sustained absence or lack of preoccupation by any boundary manager may cause the other levels to collapse in on themselves and so create confusions of roles and boundaries.

But this creates another more complex question. How does the person 'managing at the boundary' still maintain a sustaining presence for staff? I came across the concept of 'pro-tainment' which I thought helped explain the importance of the need for 'psychological presence':

> This is containment that can communicate the pleasures of self-discovery and discovery of the world and encouragement for exploration and curiosity. This is a kind of joie de vivre and links to what Lacan (1977) called 'jouissance' and Hirschorn (1997) has called 'flow'. This containment can be about making an object alive and present and promoting lively interaction with it. (Huffington 2004:66)

Pro-tainment provides a conceptual framework for addressing this sense of a 'lively presence' with others, akin to the more commonly used concept of 'holding the child in mind'.

Managing absence also necessitates the proper delegation of authority, as well as the cultural sharing of 'pro-tainment', with each person being perceived, it is hoped, as 'a lively presence'. As I have previously explored, at the Mulberry Bush School, in the absence of a manager, their deputy will 'act up'. This principle applies 'up-line'. The role of the CMG members at these times is to maintain oversight of their task areas, or delegate to an effective deputy. In this sense, there is an in-built structure which allows for both 'vertical' and collective 'horizontal' authority.

PROVIDING EMOTIONAL HOLDING AND CONTAINMENT

In the absence of the psycho-social containment of the organisation, staff morale is affected and acted out, for example by splitting, blurring of boundaries, and increased absence through illness (Miller 1989). Children will act out their heightened perception of a lack of containment through escalating destructive behaviours. These may include attacks on adults, other children and the fabric of the environment.

As stated above, I believe there is a link between the high levels of preoccupation for the task that CMG managers display and the safe functioning of the organisation. This is not a claim for any controlling or 'omnipotent' oversight, but an attuned psychological state of mind akin to what Donald Winnicott observed when he engaged in mother–baby observations and later called 'primary maternal pre-occupation' (Winnicott 1958). In this attuned state of mind, one's internal resources are in service to the task (meeting the needs of the child), and attuned to the changing dynamic atmosphere of each moment and day.

In this respect, managers, through projective identification, can often feel as though they are 'holding the baby'. Interventions by the director into the direct work are quite rare, and this has been a decision that has been developed and collectively supported to ensure the director works at the boundary, to maintain the containing and integrating function.

Theme 2: Holding the baby and managing the mess

A basic premise within our work is that the work of relationship-building parallels the mother–baby dyadic relationship. This idea was formulated by the founder of the Mulberry Bush School, Barbara Dockar-Drysdale, in her concept of the core residential task being 'the provision of primary experience' (Dockar-Drysdale 1990).

This concept is translated into practice by everyone involved in the care and education of each child, the treatment team, working together to provide a collective oversight and integration of work to facilitate each child's social and emotional growth and educational attainment. Each child (via the medium of their household and class groups) has their needs met through an individualised therapeutic experience of care and education within consistent and reliable group-based routines. Due to their impulsive and aggressive actions, the children also need caring but unsentimental experiences of robust behaviour management.

Over the course of each three-year placement, through the internalising of this nurturing and emotionally (and physically) containing experience of relationships, the child starts to feel that the adults around them are genuinely able to 'hold them in mind'. So, by staff exercising their personal authority through the 'institutional' authorisation of the treatment team and school community, the children placed at the school, who initially present themselves through chaotic and challenging behaviours and an inability to share group experiences, start to become more emotionally integrated.

Like the dyadic relationship, this work requires intense preoccupation and attunement. Through the unconscious processes of projection, frequent aggressive behaviours and by generally emanating and expressing their inner chaos, mistrust and insecurity, the children get 'inside the heads' and 'under the skin' of adults.

As with the nursing parent, this work of 'managing the mess' can be physically and emotionally draining. Workers can feel very isolated as they attempt both to meet the apparently insatiable emotional needs caused by gross deprivation, and manage the waves of demands as the children struggle to communicate these needs. Hence the need for close teamwork in supporting each worker, to ensure that there is a 'horizontal axis' of support across and with the team members, so that the individual worker does not get isolated nor unconsciously enmeshed with the child.

More key tasks
FILTERING AND MANAGING BUREAUCRATIC IMPINGEMENT

Following the analogy of the boundary as a 'filter' to the enterprise, the terms 'dynamic administration' and 'running interference' are useful descriptions of the function and experience of those working at the boundary position to 'keep out' or restrict bureaucracy that would affect the preoccupation of those working directly in close relationships with the children.

The basic principle evolves out of the Winnicottian concept of the parental roles. For Winnicott in the post-war 1950s concept of the nuclear family, this meant the mother providing the 'inner circle' of close nurture to the baby, and the father providing the 'outer circle' of support and protection for the mother and her newborn child. This was later adapted by Dockar-Drysdale to explain the need to protect the child placed within the boundary of the school from too much external 'stimuli' or unwanted 'impingement' by external forces and influences.

Parents, carers and residential workers, especially those working with younger children, know intuitively and instinctively what is 'too much' for a small child in any situation and liable to send a child 'into a wobble'.

Reeves (2001) refers to the paternal function implied in this role. Since the 1980s, residential provision, schools and children's homes in the UK have had to manage an array of new legislation and guidance from external agencies, the most recent being the impact of the Ofsted regulatory regime, with the delivery of the residential task being measured against the National Minimum and Children's Homes Quality Standards.

These external agencies expect high levels of accountability for the safety and welfare of children. In this respect, they represent one aspect of the role of 'external reality' and can provide a 'pulling force' that requires both a new 'transparency' and more attention to the internal structures of the organisation. In this way, they can both help support and develop the task. The other side of the coin is that they can also feel like unnecessary and persecutory intrusions into the task.

Over this same timeframe, societal culture has seen a gradual shift away from collective endeavours to that of individual consumerism. We have also been appropriated into a target-setting and outcomes culture, which, at worst, demands increasing accountability, but encourages over-protective and even defensive practices. The risk inherent in this culture is that the beneficial relational aspects of the task may become diluted by too many regulations, leaving little or no space for the importance of creativity, spontaneity and experiential learning.

KEEPING TO THE VISION AND NAVIGATING THE ROUTE

This is probably the most existential of the tasks. In an organisation that is 'always becoming', there is responsibility on the leadership to have a developmental vision for the future, and to have some idea of how to navigate the route in order to arrive at the destination or 'future state'.

At the Mulberry Bush School, this has been important to enable both the improvement and growth of our specialist task. More recently, this has also been influenced by our learning from the various practitioner-led research projects we have engaged with, as well as continuing to deliver the primary task in its definition as 'the task the enterprise must perform in order to survive'.

There are two different models of change management. I would suggest that they can be overlain or used independently, as each are suitable for different tasks:

- Step change: this implies a very structured linear progression which does not deviate from the desired delivery of an outcome. Projects are usually delivered in planned phases.

- Organic growth: this implies more of an evolutionary process. There might be clear vision of the desired 'future state', but this vision may be modified by changing circumstances, including realities like the money available. In a 'human services' environment like residential child care, the client group comes first, and the ability of the client group to tolerate and cope with a changing environment is an important factor that has to be taken into account.

It is possible and sometimes necessary to integrate the two models, for example our recent decision to build a six-bedded children's home and family-finding service on our site. As well as the financial planning and implications, and the phased construction of the building works, we have had to attend to the massive cultural changes and training expectations that are required as we move to operating our whole service site under the Ofsted Children's Homes Quality Standards. This major change also required the development of new roles to ensure the safety and welfare of children and staff across 52 weeks of the year.

The vision and end goal were clear: a step change to a new extended service, but navigating the route required attention to a range of other, more complex and organic processes.

There is always a creative tension between maintaining the task of the school in the here and now and working towards an improved version of the task to arrive at the future state. Working through our own internal individual group and community anxieties and resistances and bringing everyone on board across the organisation is essential if the project is to have good foundations.

Conclusion

I have tried to explore and articulate some of the concepts that I believe are central to the complexity of the demanding roles of management and leadership in therapeutic environments.

I hope that I have conveyed a belief in a more democratic, less hierarchical, structure in which any person at any level in the organisation is able to be their own manager, and equally empowered to take up leadership roles in any given situation.

I have used two themes:

- Management at the boundary as a way for staff members to orientate themselves in relation to their work; to be aware of when they are working inside or outside their task areas, and when to return to the boundary.

- The need for 'holding the baby' in relation to the tasks of emotional holding and containment.

Finally, I have explored the key tasks which I would argue are important requisites to inhabit and enact a management or leadership position within a therapeutic environment.

CHAPTER 10

FOSTERING AND POST-ADOPTION

Christine Bradley

Introduction

The provision of adequate foster homes for children and young people is an ongoing concern, with recognition of the need for the provision of substitute care being crucial to children's well-being where their home and family environment cannot meet their needs. The work of Thomas Barnardo, Thomas Bowman Stephenson and Thomas Coram during the 19th century came about through their concerns for children they found living in destitution and misery in the Victorian era in England. This influenced and embodied a change in the way that society thought about helping deprived children and young people. They formed charities with the support of philanthropic backers, which lay the foundation stone for the provision of foster homes, evolving to meet the needs of deeply traumatised and deprived children. Such was the level of their commitment, the organisations they formed continued to evolve, influencing current thinking and the development of fostering services and residential care in the UK.

Throughout the 20th and 21st centuries, we have seen the profession achieve more and more recognition, its impact increasingly understood at a deeper level and with greater significance. Fostering as a professional discipline has acquired a stronger and wider perspective about the task in hand. This evolution has also been helped by legislation (the Children Act 1989; Guidance and Regulations, Volume 4, Fostering Services; the Care Standards Act 2000; the Adoption and Children Act 2002; the Children Act 2004;

and the Children and Young Persons Act 2008) concerning the role of fostering. The number of organisations offering foster carers the support and consultation they require has grown since 1965 and has achieved a growing awareness, drawing on the work of Bowlby and Winnicott, about the impact of emotional deprivation and trauma on the lives of children and young people. Their work has informed an understanding of attachment and the behaviour of children in foster care. Today there are approximately 65,000 children requiring foster care on a short- or long-term basis, and 4000 children in the process of being adopted (Ayre *et al.* 2016).

A child's transition from one foster placement to another is common. Although the child on the surface presents as being able to adapt, inside they anticipate a repetitive cycle of the placement breaking down and needing to move on. In order for the placement to be successful, the child needs to settle into their new home environment, and in time attach to their foster parents. The carers need help and support to reach an understanding of the child's anxieties and how they can respond to these. Williams (2002:39) described a child who found it difficult to settle into a new placement:

> He felt much more comfortable in a known situation, confronted with somebody whom he did not value, someone who could be no good and no use to him, somebody not to be trusted. This was a dimension in which he moved with great ease, a very familiar one. He had not really trusted anybody in his life, and was not prepared to take chances.

In order for foster parents to deepen their understanding of how to respond to the difficult-to-manage behaviour in children and young people who are placed with them, they require appropriate support, supervision and training from others. This enables them to develop the emotional strength and level of insight needed to remain in a position where they can manage the panic and rage often projected on to them by the child. At times, such work can be painful and difficult for the foster parent, and as the American psychoanalyst Bruno Bettelheim in his work on the treatment of emotionally damaged children stated, 'Love is not enough' (1971). Emotionally fragmented children and young people whose early experiences have been consumed by feelings of emotional and physical abandonment, hostility and abuse have no sense of being loved for themselves. There has to be a new starting point in their lives, where they can accept and take in positive responses from others. This can be reached through the provision and continuity of care from their foster parents.

Many children and young people in foster care cannot make attachment relationships, as their primary attachment left them overwhelmed with feelings of panic, rage and anxiety which could not be thought about or expressed. This occurred because their first primary attachment left them feeling emotionally abandoned rather than held in the mind of their primary carer. As a consequence, they cannot bear to think about or express their emotions, and their expectation of a new relationship as they begin to attach to their current foster parent is shaped by their anxiety that early traumas could be repeated. The expectation of a repetition brings with it a level of knowing based on the child's experience, whereas the unpredictability of forming a new relationship is fraught with risk and insecurity.

Emond, Steckley and Roesch-Marsh describe this situation as follows:

> This has been called the child's internal working model of relationships. We too have an internal working model that guides our behaviour and shapes what we might expect from others. As carers our internal working model and the internal working model belonging to the child we care for can sometimes be at odds. (2016:25)

If the child remains in an emotional state of unintegration, they cannot see themselves as a separate person and they continue to seek out the primary merger that they did not experience as an infant. The infant who has experienced multiple trauma during their primary attachment experience finds it difficult to re-attach to others. They will attempt to break the relationship down destructively or self-destructively from the outset.

According to Schofield and Beek (2014), children have the capacity to form multiple relationships if they are capable of trusting their new foster parents. However, we must also recognise that to help some children reach the stage of forming attachment relationships with new parental figures they need to have some experience of a previous attachment which was good enough, acknowledging that the attachment broke down before they could develop a secure base of their own. What does this mean for the unattached and unintegrated child entering a new foster placement?

Integration and unintegration

It is never easy for a child to enter a new placement. Their expectations about what to expect from the family will differ according to their previous experiences of a family placement. Some will be able to face the reality of their new situation; others will create a fantasy about the new situation, masking a painful reality of their experience of abuse and hostility which influences their reaction to the foster parents.

The level of their integrated or unintegrated state will form their response to the transition from one home to another. The unintegrated child becomes overwhelmed with fears of abandonment, because they did not experience a sense of absolute dependence with their primary carer. Without a secure sense of self being internalised, there is no foundation from which they can form relationships. Their inner world is framed by feelings of trauma, hostility and abuse, which makes relating to the outside world unthinkable and unbearable for them. To survive, they create a split between their inner-world experiences and the new reality of their placement. Consequently, they can find it difficult to understand and relate to the reality they are living with. They can find transitions from one part of their life to the next stage impossible to manage. For some, the only way to survive their current reality of managing alternative placements is through blocking their early experiences from their mind. This influences how a child will benefit and make use of the care offered to them in the new foster home. The difficulty is that they could easily feel attacked by the outside world, which could lead them to act out their unbearable feelings, with serious consequences.

The unintegrated child needs to have a period with their foster parents where they feel they are being taken care of as an infant or small child, an experience which became lost or fragmented in their early years. During the initial period of their placement, they may require more primary provision than emotional support. If the foster carer can find a way of relating to the lost child in their inner world, it could provide them with the emotional resources needed to support their maturational development.

The unintegrated child could appear as charming and compliant, but not able to communicate in real terms. They attempt to fall into collusive and seductive relationships with carers; they cannot learn from their experiences and are likely to show intense and powerful emotional difficulties, resulting in them acting out what they cannot bear to think about. Even with the help of carers or workers, the unintegrated child cannot accept personal responsibility for their actions. When they become destructive or self-destructive, they show little capacity to repair the damage they have caused and no concern for others.

The emotionally integrated child in need of foster care has most likely experienced trauma and abusive experiences throughout their earlier childhood, but because of having the benefit of a period of good enough primary experiences, there is a strong possibility they will be able to form attachment relationships with their carers. The underlying reasoning for this is that they have reached a starting point from which they can emotionally develop. Importantly, reality can be thought about, and, with support, they can learn from their experiences. Since they have achieved the capacity to show concern, empathy and remorse towards others, they have internalised a secure sense of self, and can express anger and sadness to their carers. With support they can work through their feelings, beginning to understand more about the reality they have to face. This support and help from their foster carers enables the child in time to create alternative attachments between themselves and their foster parents.

The integrated child has a sense of being a person who is developing their own sense of self. It is acknowledged that at times they can become very fragile and regress to their original feelings about themselves. At these points, they are likely to have powerful temper tantrums, but with help and support from their carers these feelings can be worked through to a point where the child begins to communicate their emotions to those who are responsible for them. With support, they can share the world with others and keep to the rules, as they have the ability to learn from experiences.

Foster parents adapting to integrated and unintegrated children in need of care

What does this mean for foster carers, who are experiencing levels of emotional unintegration and integration from the children and young people they are responsible for? They will find themselves opening up to a multitude of emotions from the children and within themselves.

As the child begins to develop a level of attachment, the carer is faced with changes in the child's behaviour. It can be difficult, painful and at times quite unbearable for foster carers to have to hold on to some powerful projections thrown at them by the child. The child's projections should be viewed as elements of transference in their relationship, where feelings of despair, hopelessness and being under threat are projected onto the carer. It is important at this point for the carer to understand, respond appropriately and not overreact or collude with their behaviour.

The following questions may help foster carers to evaluate the inner-world projections of the child and how these can be managed:

- What are the areas in the child's life when they can function? What is the end result of their functioning? How do they express their feelings, and do you respond or react to their behaviour?

- What are the areas of the day when they are not able to function at all? How do you respond when the child's capacity to function breaks down?

- Think about a child or young person you have been with or are currently responsible for. How do they make you feel after spending time with them? If they brought up a strong feeling in you, what did that represent? How much of the feeling in you came from the child or young person? Did the emotion touch a feeling in you?

By reflecting on what the child brings up for the foster parent could also be a sign of what is happening in their inner world. If they make you panic or feel very sad and angry, it could represent what the feeling means to them. It is possible that, with some insight and understanding to help the child reach a stage in their maturational development, they can begin to integrate their own experiences and develop a stronger sense of self.

Responding to the child's behaviour

Having recognised the strong feeling which has been projected onto you from the child or young person's internal world, and identified what it represents, try responding to them by saying: 'Because I have been left feeling very sad after being with you, it suggests to me that you may be feeling a strong sense of sadness which you have never been able to speak about. I am wondering, what can I do to help you feel a little better?'

Only make the statement if it feels like a right and natural communication for the child to receive from you. Maintain the awareness of responding to the child rather than reacting. The foster parent's response shows the child that you are thinking about them; to react is a defensive action from the carer and can make the child feel that you are attacking them, leaving the possibility for them to create more destructive behaviour.

The following is an example of how the emotional need assessment programme can help a foster carer to understand and manage a child or young person's complex behaviour patterns.

■ EMOTIONAL NEED ASSESSMENT: MOLLY

Background

Molly is seven-and-a-half years of age. Her mother had been diagnosed with mental health problems, drug abuse and self-harming. She was self-absorbed in her own emotional needs and had little time or concern for Molly or her sisters. Her father had expressed little interest in Molly either.

Molly has been in her current foster placement for six months after the previous one broke down because of her behaviour, which they found unmanageable. The foster parents have two other foster children, although they have a very committed relationship to Molly. She in turn is very needy, unable to let the foster mother out of her sight. A critical incident has led the foster parents to feel a deep concern about Molly. This has led their support workers to suggest that an emotional need assessment programme could help the family to find a way forward in their care and commitment to her and provide them with a deeper understanding as to how they can manage her difficult behaviour.

Molly has recently exhibited destructive and difficult behaviour. The most serious of her actions has been that in a fit of envy, anger and rage towards the other foster children in the home, Molly killed their pet hamsters, but not her own. She is not able to show any guilt or concern about her behaviour, nor can she show any attempt to make reparation for her actions.

On discussing Molly and her past experiences, it appears that she is functioning at the level of an unintegrated child. Her early mother–child relationship broke down before she was ready to separate, and she received traumatic and hostile experiences, creating a high level of anxiety for her to manage, which felt quite unbearable. It has left her not ready to emotionally develop a sense of self that she feels comfortable with. Instead, it has resulted in her developmental progress not being maintained and not evolving. As she has grown, her feelings of emotional abandonment have created a sense of 'panic and rage' in her, which she cannot express, so instead she resorts to 'acting out' her emotions instead. This makes it difficult for Molly to manage her behaviour and to hold on to meaningful attachment relationships with her carers. She is in danger of breaking down and acting out her emotions towards her foster parents, which may lead to her possible attachment relationship with them being in danger of breaking down.

The following three aspects of Molly's day-to-day living experiences are discussed in the emotional need assessment:

- boundaries

- containing emotion, anxiety, anger and stress

- play.

Boundaries

Question: Is Molly able to manage boundaries practically, physically and emotionally and is she able to show a sense of personal responsibility?

Response of the foster parents and social worker: With strong support Molly can manage practical boundaries, but she cannot manage those relating to her personal or physical life. Her inner world is filled with anxieties and uncertainties and she cannot yet make a meaningful attachment with another person, as she is not yet ready to share her world with others. Her sense of self is emotionally very fragile at times, and she finds it difficult to manage stressful situations. The danger is that she might break down, disrupting the world around her through her destructive behaviour. She felt emotionally abandoned by her mother in her early years, and in order to survive she has become her own caretaker. Molly had to take care of herself in order to survive and became emotionally buried within her inner world.

Syndrome: Molly is assessed as functioning at the level of a caretaker child with aspects of her which have become emotionally frozen.

Therapeutic treatment plan

- There is a part of Molly which functions as an 18-month-old child, when her mother was not able to take care of her, so she became her own caretaker self, freezing her emotions. Her foster parents need to let her become absolutely dependent on them, allowing her to hand the caretaker over to them and leaving her space for her 'little self' who needs taking care of by the foster parents to come to the fore.

- The primary needs of her 'little self' that remain locked inside her need to be recognised and provided for by the foster parents.

- All primary provision offered to Molly should be within a very clear structure.

Containing emotion, anxiety, anger and stress

Question: Can Molly contain emotions, or does she act out destructively or self-destructively?

Response of the foster parents and social worker: Molly presents a feeling of despair and sadness. Her emotional fragility and her belief that the outside world is too difficult and painful for her to reach out to leaves her feeling constantly emotionally raw. To survive Molly has developed her own fantasy world, which has become her reality. Currently she ignores the consequences of her behaviour and finds it difficult to regret the outcome of her behaviour or make reparation for her actions.

In this section, Molly is assessed as being emotionally frozen. Throughout her early life she has been overwhelmed with unbearable feelings of panic and rage, which were neither recognised nor addressed by her carers. It is possible for the frozen aspects of Molly's behaviour to 'thaw' to a point where she will be more able to express concern and guilt if her carers can acknowledge and 'bear the unbearable' emotions which have become embedded in her inner world.

Therapeutic treatment plan

- A frozen child cannot manage the intimacy of attachment relationships. Her carers need to adapt to her dependency needs through small aspects of her day-to-day living.

- Her small areas of functioning need to be valued and supported. Do not be too reactive when the slightest stress results in her breaking down and ceasing to function.

- Molly needs to be constantly held in the mind of her foster parents. She did not experience being held in the mind of her mother in her early life and consequently she constantly needs to realise they are thinking about her.

- Adapting to her primary needs can be through the provison of special food, a story being read to her like a two-year-old, or providing her with an experience where she feels thought about by the parents.

Play

Question: Does she engage in solitary or co-operative play? Is she easily distracted or sometimes disruptive?

Response of the foster parents and social worker: Molly cannot play on her own with pleasure, nor does play have a significant meaning for her. In group play she can become very disruptive and prevent others from playing. She needs as many opportunities for infantile play provided for her as possible.

Diagnosis: Frozen

Therapeutic treatment plan

- Molly needs to have a special play time with one of her foster parents. Once a time is agreed, it is important that it continues. The continuity of good experiences is very important for Molly, if she is to develop a sense of trust with her foster parents.

- Molly needs some tactile play consisting of sand, water or clay-making out of which she could create an object which could hold some meaning for her.

- Molly can be helped to become attached to one toy, which will always be there for her to hold. This forms the beginning of making an attachment to an object which carries meaning for her (transitional object).

- As Molly finds it difficult to communicate verbally, it could be that her play experiences provide an opportunity for the foster parents to communicate symbolically with her.

Four months later: assessment conclusions

The emotional need assessment has concluded that Molly is functioning at the stage of pre-attachment known as unintegration. Her syndrome has been assessed as being at the level of a caretaker child, with aspects which remain emotionally frozen. For the foster parents to help her to reach the stage of emotional integration, i.e. becoming a person in her own right and as an individual, they will need to follow the therapeutic treatment programme over a period of four months. Asking them to bear the feelings of hopelessness and helplessness which are embedded in Molly's inner world and helping her to move towards experiencing the outside world with hope, joy and a sense of creativity will not be an easy task for them, but is possible to achieve. They are committed to helping Molly reach the next stage of her life, and prepared to undertake as much support and provision for her as is necessary to emotionally enable her to take a greater sense of personal responsibility for her own behaviour.

A follow-up emotional need assessment is undertaken on Molly four months later. The foster parents have followed through the therapeutic treatment programme. At the meeting, they are feeling far more hopeful about Molly's placement and have seen a number of positive changes in her behaviour and in her relationship towards them. The questions originally discussed about Molly's day-to-day living in the previous assessment are re-evaluated.

Boundaries

Outcomes: The foster parents consistently follow the treatment plan, holding Molly in their minds, regardless of her difficult behaviour. Their response gives her a strong feeling of emotional containment. Because she is developing a secure base to live from, this is guiding her towards being able to think about her behaviour more. Molly has expressed deep concern and regret about the killing of the hamsters, and has made an attempt to make reparation for her behaviour. She is no longer so overwhelmed with destructive and self-destructive feelings, although she does need a great deal of support and provision, but is more able to hold on to boundaries, emotionally, physically and practically.

Containing emotion, anxiety, anger and stress

Outcomes: According to her foster parents, although Molly can be emotionally quite raw at times, she feels safer in the home environment, practically, physically and emotionally, because of their developing relationship with her. She is also more able to express herself and communicate about her anxieties than previously. They experience Molly's emotional world as feeling less intense than previously, and this makes their relationship with her less fraught.

Play

Outcomes: The previous need assessment stated that Molly needed to acquire a sense of absolute dependence on her foster parents. In her play with the foster mother, she needed to experience her as being totally preoccupied throughout the play experience with her. This is very time-consuming for the foster mother, but she is prepared to go through consistently responding to Molly's play needs. The result of her maternal preoccupation is that Molly now asks to play with the foster mother for a short period and can then continue playing on her own individually with particular play materials. Molly is now beginning to use 'transitional' play as she starts to acquire her own sense of self. She is also beginning to move from being at the stage of absolute dependence on her foster parents towards one of interdependence, hence her ability to play on her own with pleasure and keep to the rules.

The second need assessment programme assessed Molly as having now moved on from the syndrome of unintegration through to a level of fragile integration. She will continue to need a great deal of emotional support and at times of stress could disintegrate and fall into pieces for a brief period. Because she is reaching a stage of emotional integration, she will not revert back to previous behaviour. She may begin to reach a level of depression when she is thinking about her life, and it could create concern for her foster parents, but as she is now ready for a period of therapy, in time difficult periods in her life could be worked through. Molly is now beginning to come together as a person and is ready to start making more positive attachment relationships.

Molly will continue to need considerable support if she is to develop her inner confidence. With support, she will be able to work through and communicate about difficult and painful periods in her day-to-day living. At times of stress she will need many opportunities for communication or she could be in danger of acting out her feelings.

As a result of the emotional need assessment and therapeutic treatment programme, Molly has developed emotionally from being unintegrated in the syndromes of frozen and caretaker child to being at the stage of emotional integration and ready to make a meaningful attachment in her relationship with her foster parents, in whom she is acquiring a sense of trust.

The use of emotional need assessments and treatment programmes by foster parents

Most foster parents will have periods during their day-to-day living with their foster children when they have great doubts as to how they can manage their emotional difficulties, while trying to understand and manage their challenging behaviour. They believe they are providing all the care and attention the child needs, only to have it thrown back at them with anger and contempt. This can leave them feeling hopeless and helpless, regardless of the love and care they are offering. At this point the work can feel quite unbearable for the foster parents, and without the support which they need, helping them to understand the reasoning for the child's behaviour, they can find themselves in the process of overreacting to the child, thus making their behaviour very difficult. It could even reach a point where the placement is in danger of breaking down and coming to an end. The outcome for such challenging behaviour is that for the child or young person it becomes yet another repetition in their lives of their compulsive behaviour, and the foster parents find they have reached a sense of despair and despondency about their role as parent figures in the child's life. The need assessment programme will provide them with support and guidance as to how they can relate to the inner world of the child, with appropriate responses.

> If a child has little value for himself, he will have little value for others. Their interactions with others can only sometimes be with empathy, and little dignity (self-worth and respect for others). With little value or self-esteem for self and others, they are not likely to ask for help, nor can they be more open with their feelings. (Oehlberg 2008:3)

However, being a foster parent is not always painful and overwhelming, and there can be moments of the child's placement when they experience what has been termed the 'wow factor' in the work. The moment when the child feels emotionally contained by the foster parents enough to hold their arms out to be held and ask to be nurtured is truly a 'golden moment' for the foster parents. It means the child has broken through their own emotional barriers and is reaching out to form an attachment in their relationship with their foster carers that carries meaning. The work can feel quite unbearable at times to the foster parents, but with help and support it can be achievable and workable.

The unintegrated child has a magnitude of missing elements in their inner world, which makes reality quite unbearable for them to manage. The foster parents, with help and support, can 'bear the unbearable' aspects of a child who, as they start to attach to their foster carers, expresses early primitive feelings which have remained embedded in their inner world. The commitment and determination of the foster parents can help the child to emotionally develop and begin to internalise their experiences as part of the family. This can then form the basis from which an attachment relationship between the child and the foster parents can start to develop. It will help them find the belief and confidence in themselves to make sense of their experiences in the outside world, and to understand what they can gain from the opportunities provided.

Living with the unintegrated child

Throughout this book, I have examined how unintegration relates to the earliest period of the infant's life, when in a state of absolute dependence on their primary carer and needing to experience a period of maternal preoccupation. This positive primary experience lays the foundation stone for the infant's maturational development and throughout their life. During the earliest part of the infant's sense of existing as a baby, their emotional needs and demands are very high as they began to develop their own sense of self. In time, they no longer require the intensity of the primary merger they experienced earlier, as they become more aware of their own sense of self. They begin to integrate their experiences, feeling more whole as a person and wanting to share their world with others.

A child who as an infant felt traumatised and abused emotionally and physically by their primary carer is left with the primitive feelings they were unable to express. It can be difficult for foster carers when the child's early primitive feelings are expressed. The foster parent can at times feel attacked, and the child's behaviour, if not understood, can feel unbearable for them to manage. If the foster parent can understand the representation of the behaviour in the child's world, it will be easier for them to respond rather than react to them. For example, an unintegrated child who is eight years of age may still be functioning emotionally like an infant. When challenged with boundaries they have to work within, they could seem like an infant who has no boundaries in their thinking. Part of the child still feels like a one-year-old, so to help them feel emotionally contained, the foster parents need to respond to both aspects of the child: the eight-year-old who is in the latency period of their development, and the lost infant who fears that nobody will be with them. When asking the child to help with clearing the dining table, the foster parent might say: 'I know that you find helping and keeping to our boundaries difficult, but it is important that we can help you to begin to become a part of us. I will help you and we will clear the table together.' This could help to prevent the child from breaking the plates and creating difficulties, as they experience the parent as responding to both aspects of their character, supporting the eight-year-old and providing for the one-year-old. With a feeling of preoccupation from their foster parents, they will slowly begin to come together and feel more complete as a person.

Transference and counter-transference in a foster home

The concept of transference and counter-transference is of help in enabling foster carers to understand the dynamics of their evolving relationships with the children they foster and to understand the nature of feelings that are transferred onto them from their foster children. This phenomenon is likely to occur as the child begins to form an attachment to them. The effects of transference and counter-transference on the parents can be difficult to manage if not understood.

Transference relates to the transfer of past unresolved feelings, conflicts and attitudes the child brings with them to their present relationships, situations and circumstances.

It could be that their unresolved early feelings precipitate behavioural and thought patterns in subsequent relationships, even though certain actions of their behaviour and their attitudes towards their reality confrontation may be inappropriate for their current interaction.

Counter-transference is a term used to describe the foster parents' reactions to the child's transferred feelings:

> the reaction set off in the worker as a result of being receptive to the child's transferred feelings. These emotions, in so far as they correctly mirror the client's, are a most helpful guide to understanding them. (Salzberger-Wittenberg 1999:18–19)

If a child transfers to the foster parent feelings and ideas that belong to previous figures in their past experiences, and behaves as though they were that person – for example, a hostile mother or an abusive father

– the experience can be bewildering. It can be painful and difficult for carers to understand and respond to the projection from the child. It could also touch emotions in the foster parent that capture the essence of certain painful and difficult experiences in their own life. To help foster parents with the transference and counter-transference aspects of their work, support and supervision are required. They also need the opportunity for reflective thought about the child for whom they are responsible. If they can deepen their own understanding about their responses to the child, and how the child's behaviour affects them, it will also help the foster parents to develop an insight and understanding about the child's behaviour. This will influence the dynamics between foster parent and child, with the child believing their relationship can become one of attachment. In time and with support, the relationship becomes stronger and their attachment will be more important to the child. As the child begins to internalise their experiences and develop a sense of self they can live with, the relationship starts to express a sense of meaning and sincerity.

It is at this point in the care and treatment of the child that the 'golden moments' can occur. The foster parent can truly experience the wow factor in their relationship with the child and the time spent with them. This is when a foster carer arrives at a stage in their care and work with their foster child of realising that the pain and hurt they have endured while being with them has paid off. The child begins to express more emotion than they originally could, and shows a sense of guilt and concern towards others and for their behaviour. That indeed is the 'golden moment' for the carers, when having to 'bear the unbearable' feels worthwhile.

Post-adoption

Placements of children through fostering and adoption services have a number of differences and similarities between them. The majority of children who are fostered or adopted have experienced significant harm and been removed from their biological family because of maltreatment.

When children's adoption takes place, they will no longer be a part of their birth family. This reality will prompt a number of emotions, ranging from excitement to relief, but also deep anxiety and expectations of hostility and abuse towards them, based on their early experiences.

The amount of disruption they experienced in their infantile years will influence their interaction with their adoptive parents. The response of the adoptive parents will be influenced by the adopted child's expectations of them. The emotional needs of adopted children can be similar to those of fostered children. It is possible that adopted children are stuck at an unintegrated stage of their development, where because of trauma in their early experiences they have little sense of self, or of being a person who can relate to others.

Similarities between foster and adoption placements

1. The patterns of behaviour in the children can be similar. The majority of them have been through traumatic infantile experiences.

2. Children who are adopted may have experienced their infantile–maternal relationship as one of abandonment, anxiety and fear. They remain in an unintegrated state, unable to make secure attachment relationships with the adoptive and foster parents.

3. Transference and counter-transference in the relationship between children and their adoptive parents can be re-enacted because of unresolved conflicts from previous experiences and will affect the relationship between the parents and the children.

4. Children in adopted or foster homes often benefit from need assessment programmes.

5. Each child can form positive or negative relationships with the foster family or adoptive parents.

6. Both adoptive parents and foster parents have certain expectations of the children.

Differences between fostering and adoptive parents

In foster families, depending on the attachment relationship made with the foster parents, there is the prospect of a temporary or permanent placement for children. The parents, have ongoing support from the fostering organisation, leaving them confident that there is always a professional who can support them, and whom they can contact if they need to do so. There are a number of positive and negative feelings the child may throw at the parents, and they find themselves experiencing a mixture of emotions. It is at this point that the parents may need professional support to enable them to use their emotions productively in their relationship with their foster child.

For adoptive parents, the reality they need to accept in their care of the children they have adopted differs from that of foster parents. The adoption process for the parents is psychologically similar to that of pregnancy. It is a unique and complex process and carries a powerful mix of emotions for them. There are many different reasons why parents make a decision to adopt a child, such as the death of a previous child of their own, not being able to have children or wanting to have additional children within their family. Whatever their reasons, the decision to adopt a child is life-changing.

There can be a gulf between the adoptive parents' expectations of the child and the reality of what they have taken on board. Post-adoption depression is a recognised factor for some placements, often occurring approximately one month after the child has been placed with the parents. However, a study has reported that there is no significant difference in the incidence of depression between adoptive and birth mothers (Senecky *et al.* 2009).

Parents who adopt an infant between 6 and 12 months old who has experienced trauma in the first six months of their life can find it difficult to comprehend that these experiences have left the child with anxiety and uncertainty. Perry stated:

> Children growing up in chaos, neglect, and threat do not have the fundamental developmental experiences required to express their underlying genetic potential to self-regulate, relate, communicate, and think. These children are undersocialized and at great risk for emotional, behavioural, social, cognitive, and physical health problems. (2006:28)

Perry explains that trauma and disruption for the infant from the womb and onwards through birth and throughout the first five years of their life does influence their maturational growth and emotional development. During that time, the brain is still developing, and although their trauma cannot be thought about, it remains within them and can be re-echoed when the reality they are living in enters a turbulent and disruptive period. This can bemuse the adoptive parents, who have been giving the child a great deal of loving care. However, as explained earlier in this chapter, if the parents can manage to accept the lost parts of the child that have become locked inside them, leaving them with a sense of despair and fury, it will be possible to help the child value the 'golden moments' they experience with their adoptive parents and begin to develop a stronger sense of being an individual and a person in their own right.

Conclusion

Throughout this chapter I have examined the complex and positive aspects of the fostering and adoption of children. I began by explaining the historical context of the profession and then discussed how much our insight and understanding about the work have grown. In recent years, neuroscience has presented us with the research and scientific evidence highlighting the impact of trauma on children in their early lives. It strengthens the work of Donald Winnicott and John Bowlby and others, whose compassion and commitment to understanding the impact of trauma on children in their developing years underpins the work and practice being understood and developed today. Bach (1972) offered an insight into the self, and addressed issues of conformity and individuality in his fable describing the life of a seagull. On the back of the book *Jonathan Livingston Seagull*, Bach wrote:

> This fable is about the importance of making the most of our lives, even if our goals run contrary to the norms of our flock, tribe or neighbourhood. Through the metaphor or flight, Jonathan's story shows us that, if we follow our dreams, we too can soar.

Fostering and adoptive parents can help the children who have come to live with them to move away from their nightmares and enjoy their dreams. This is where the 'golden moments' can make life more bearable for them, as they begin to reach out to what they can gain from family life – the new experiences to which they have not previously had access or been able to take in before.

CHAPTER 11

THE UNINTEGRATED ADOLESCENT

Christine Bradley

Within this book, we have examined the concept of integration and unintegration in the emotional development of children and young people. This chapter will examine the impact of early childhood traumas on the maturational development of the adolescent. We will discuss how abuse, neglect and hostility can be repeated, leading to cycles of destructive and self-destructive behaviours, impacting on the young person's sense of self and blocking their emotional, sexual and social development from healthy maturation. The adolescent is viewed mainly as an individual entering an emotional stage where they grapple with the transition from early childhood through to adulthood and deal with the pressures and challenges of the reality they have to face. In order for the child to become a person with their own personal identity, which they have learned to value, key factors must be addressed. Access to education offers opportunities for developing new identities, economic security, personal self-esteem and the realisation of talents.

Cameron, Connelly and Jackson wrote:

The education of children in care is at long last in the foreground of policy attention. Success in education is still one of the main means of prosperity as an adult. Being without educational qualifications or the wherewithal to attain them leaves young people highly vulnerable to unemployment and poverty as well as ill-health and diminished self-esteem. Ensuring young people in its care are educated is one of the most effective actions the state can take to prevent them from further risks as adults and improve their quality of life. (2015:8)

The following statistics outlined by Ayre *et al.* (2016) present a context and give an indication of the breadth of the situation:

> The Children's Society (2016) reported that 10,830 young people left care aged 16 or over in England last year, an increase of over 40% in the last decade (Keep On Caring, 2016). Approximately 39% of care leavers aged between 19–21 are 'not in education, employment or training' (NEET), 49% of men under 21 who have come into contact with the criminal justice system have had a care experience, while 25% of people experiencing homelessness have spent time in care (NAO, 2015).

The above reminds us of the complexity of the classroom situation and highlights the impact of challenging behaviour, poor engagement in the learning process, underachievement and the inadequacy of the teacher's understanding of the unintegrated adolescent.

The core issue for the child in the classroom setting is for them to feel safe within an environment that is secure, reliable and predictable. Teachers need to be aware that emotionally fragmented adolescents find change painful and difficult to manage, but with security, they are able to thrive. However, sudden changes of teachers on whom they were depending, and who made them feel safe, noticed, respected and accepted, can shatter an adolescent's security. It is only when an unintegrated child feels safe and calm in the classroom that they can begin to relate to and think about their learning. This is a difficult task for the teacher, but it is crucial for them to understand that for their teaching to be successful with emotionally fragmented adolescents, they need to provide a well-structured environment which includes a level of creative thinking that reaches out to the development of the self in the classroom setting. Episodes of acting out can occur in the classroom, disrupting children's learning if teachers do not have the ability to consider the management of the change and the subsequent reaction of the pupils.

Winnicott (1965:87) makes an interesting point about adolescent transition that takes place during this period, noting that there is a period when, to feel real, they have to survive the depression which he refers to as 'struggling to get through the doldrums'.

So what does this mean for the child, who throughout their adolescence is left in an emotionally unintegrated state which blocks their maturational development?

We are now aware as adults that adolescence is a difficult and at times painful process for those who are developing from a child to a young person. The adolescent who has been traumatised continually throughout their infancy and early childhood is left unable to express their powerful emotions of panic and rage. They have a 'disconnect' within their sense of being alive, and are unable to build a bridge between their inner world and the external reality. Their experiences of emotional isolation and early abandonment have made it difficult for them to relate to others effectively and to make healthy and meaningful personal relationships with individuals or groups. Their need to identify with others becomes more aligned with groups who are linked into the roots of the anti-social tendency.

Children whose inner world has become infiltrated with fears and anxieties feel overwhelmed and helpless and are vulnerable and at extreme risk. If not helped to work through their anxieties and fears, they continue to experience life through patterns of behaviour that can be destructive or self-destructive (Bradley 1997). When this pattern of challenging behaviour is allowed to continue uninterrupted by the adult, their compulsion to repeat abusive and challenging behaviour continues. This survival mechanism can take on perverse and more primitive forms of behaviour, and can lead the adolescent to engage in the anti-social tendency, which becomes their functioning reality. Dealing with these patterns of destructive and self-destructive behaviour that become established requires the skill, commitment, knowledge and insight of carers and other professionals who can withstand the child's despair to enable them to live a shared reality with other people.

Sadly, there is no 'magic cure' for the pain and hurt that adolescents have suffered in their early years. Professionals, carers and parents seek ways of supporting and providing for the adolescent, which helps them to feel more comfortable with themselves, to experience moments of peace and achievement and to begin to view a way forwards in their life that feels sufficiently satisfying and that they can hold on to and internalise as good experiences. This allows their sense of self to become stronger and feel more real. Without this happening and during periods of stress, they can feel at 'war' between themselves and the outside world, resorting to destructive and self-destructive patterns of behaviour, over-identifying with the anti-social tendency and attacking others. Winnicott, describing the anti-social tendency, wrote:

At the root of the antisocial tendency there is always a deprivation. The antisocial child is searching in some way or other, violently or gently, to get the world to acknowledge its debt: or is trying to make the world re-inform the framework which got broken up. (1965:86)

Unintegrated adolescents, whose early traumas left them having to survive unbearable and unthinkable anxieties, have disassociated themselves from the expectations others have about their behaviour. To survive they have found ways of denying their pain, presenting a false self to others. This is not akin to their inner world of emotions, which remain trapped inside them at a primitive level of thinking and expression. It is possible that this can result in either severe depression and despair, or a series of destructive or self-destructive acting out, as they have little sense of personal responsibility for these behaviours or their impact on others.

The following exchange describes how profoundly isolated, sad and lost an unintegrated adolescent can feel if not recognised by others.

Mark, 14 years old, was waiting for me as I stepped out of my car when I arrived at the Caldecott Community. He looked sad and lost. 'How many cars do you have, Christine?' he asked me. Responding to the lack of aliveness in his face, I said, 'Seven. I have three Rolls-Royces, two Daimlers, a helicopter and a horse and cart.' 'Where do you keep them all?' he asked. 'In my imagination,' I replied. 'What do you keep in your imagination?' He breathed a deep sigh. 'I don't have any imagination, I only have the reality I live with.' 'That is a shame,' I responded. 'Why is it a shame?' he asked. 'Because with an imagination, reality does not seem so hard.' 'Reality has always been hard,' replied Mark. 'May I have some of your imagination?' he asked me. 'Of course,' I said. 'You may have the use of one of my Rolls-Royces.' 'Thank you,' he said, 'now I feel a little better.'

Mark made me realise that if we are to help the unintegrated adolescent to move away from their despair and sense of emotional isolation, we have to be prepared to reach out to the lost and traumatised child who lies within them. There are parts of the unintegrated adolescent that need providing for and responding to by their workers or carers, while at the same time the young person must be offered sufficient ego support to help them to continue functioning as an adolescent.

The integrated adolescent can manage their life experiences which, although at times may be painful and difficult, can be worked through effectively, enabling them to become emotionally stronger.

- Although they challenge others, this occurs in a setting in which need for dependence is met.

- They test society's boundaries while also being able to learn from these experiences.

In contrast, the emotionally unintegrated adolescent:

- is unable to seek out relationships in which they are interdependent with because they have never experienced an early sense of absolute dependence with trusted carers and seek to merge with others

- lives within their own created reality, using destructive or self-destructive behavior to survive. It is difficult to help them to learn from their experiences because they are unable to accept responsibility within their own reality as it does not concur with the demands of the external reality

- views the outside world as hostile and attacking them. Unintegrated adolescents cannot challenge society and learn from these experiences; instead they engage in the anti-social tendency as they are unable to think about the consequence of their behavior.

Public incidences of adolescents using their levels of emotional integration and unintegration to manage the challenges and complexities of society, and the impact their behaviour has on the cultural population they live alongside, differ. Adolescents who are emotionally integrated can make their voice and convictions heard en masse through the ballot box, voting to bring about political change. In contrast, unintegrated adolescents may be more likely to use violence towards people or their belongings – stealing from individuals or acting destructively towards their vehicles, homes or other buildings in an attempt to express their anger and disaffection from society. An adolescent who remains at an unintegrated stage of development is emotionally fragile and at times quite vulnerable to groups who carry powerful and intense destructive tendencies with them. They find the consequences of their acting out or destructiveness towards others very difficult to acknowledge and accept. However, we must also realise that it is quite possible with appropriate care and treatment for the unintegrated adolescent to develop and strengthen their sense of self, coming together as an individual and moving towards emotional integration. They can be helped to start to find a purpose for their living which carries meaning and can be creative and developmental.

Adolescence is a difficult process for anyone developing from a child into a young person. What are the implications for the adolescent who remains unintegrated?

Trowell (2011) refers to the work of Mo and Eagle Laufer in pointing out that a developmental view of adolescence should not be underestimated and its link to early childhood experiences recognised, noting that a real possibility for change can be achieved when working with young people by re-actualising their struggle towards integration.

Table 11.1 outlines the differences and similarities for adolescents when they face the challenges of emotional transition from childhood through adolescence and into young adulthood.

Table 11.1: Differences and similarities for adolescents in the emotional transition from childhood to adulthood

Adolescent process	Integrated adolescent	Unintegrated adolescent
Childhood to adulthood, separation and individuation	Adolescence is the period when the parent–child relationship changes in character and the identity of the self is formed. In order to achieve individuation, the adolescent has to let go of the internalised childhood image of the parent. The adolescent who experienced a secure base with their primary carer has arrived at a certain stage of maturational development. There is a sense of self they need to work with to develop. Adolescence will still be an uphill 'struggle through the doldrums' as Winnicott stated. However, integrated adolescents can see and think about the reality they are experiencing and learn how to manage their difficulties.	Because their infantile and early childhood experiences were experienced as traumatic for them, they were left floundering in 'bits and pieces' around their identity. Their sense of self remains fragile. Because they did not experience a level of absolute dependence on their primary carer, they continually seek to merge with others in their adolescence. Because they could not internalise a secure attachment in early childhood which they could not begin to build on, they continue to seek out adolescence relationships on which they can be absolutely dependent. The unintegrated adolescent finds it difficult to integrate any good experience they are offered. Because their self-esteem is so low, they do not believe they deserve anything that is good and real in their life.

| Emotional development | Emotional development is the growth in the child's ability to distinguish between themselves and others and to express their emotions in socially acceptable ways. They can also understand themselves in socially acceptable ways, and the emotional content of other people's communication.

Adolescents who are emotionally integrated can learn from their experiences if they make a mistake. They will experience depressive episodes about their life, but with help and support can work through their sad and painful emotions. Reality becomes difficult and at times unbearable for them, but they carry enough sense of self to be able to find their place in society and understand how to make it work. When they express powerful emotions, they are ones of anger, sadness and loss, which can be worked through and thought about. | The unintegrated adolescent, whether they are at the level of frozen, archipelago, caretaker or fragile integration, find managing emotions very difficult, because they were not able to express them in their infantile and early childhood years. Instead, they remain stuck in more primitive emotions of panic, rage and unthinkable anxiety and, because they cannot be thought about, they remain embedded in their inner world at a primitive level. These emotions explode and come out of the adolescent's inner world like a thunderstorm that takes over their environment and drenches those around them.

This can result in destructive and self-destructive behaviour being acted out by them. It can influence their capacity to feel emotionally contained, resulting in them ceasing to function in the outside world, feeling attacked and let down by others who live there. It can lead them to act out their emotions with dire consequences. |

cont.

Adolescent process	Integrated adolescent	Unintegrated adolescent
Relationships with individuals and groups	Most adolescents who are emotionally integrated do carry traumatic experiences with them. They will start to separate from their maternal relationship, searching to find their own. They can form important relationships as they feel like an individual in their own right. Although they will disagree and argue, they will also hold on to a feeling of 'keeping on going'. As they become a part of group activity, it will help them to find their own voice to express their view about reality and how it works. They carry a sense of group and personal responsibility for their actions. The development of a range of relationships is part of adolescence, within which is the forming of intimate relationships. This involves not only sex, but caring and sharing oneself with another person, within a reciprocal relationship.	Unintegrated adolescents find holding on to relationships with others difficult to achieve. Their need to create a sense of 'absolute dependence' in their relationship could make it difficult for the other person involved. They find it difficult to be part of a group and keep to the rules. In adolescence, they are in danger of joining groups that focus on the anti-social tendency, becoming over-identified with them. Alternatively, their emotional fragility can place them in danger of being used and abused by groups that are searching for adolescents who will allow themselves to be taunted by them. The unintegrated adolescent is vulnerable to risk-taking behaviours, grooming and exploitation in their seeking for love and security. Their experience of abnormal behaviours as infants and young children may provide a 'known security' which they may seek to replicate as adolescents.

The journey from childhood to adolescence and adulthood can be a long and arduous one. There can be periods of good fun and happiness but equally times where the young person is overrun by despair, sadness and an overriding feeling of futility. Winnicott wrote:

> The morality of adolescence goes much deeper than wickedness, and has its motto. 'To thine own self be true.' The adolescent is engaged in trying to find the self to be true to. This is linked with the fact that the cure for adolescence is the passage of time. (1990:146)

Because this period of time is one which must be lived. It is essentially a time of personal discovery. Each individual is engaged in a living experience, a problem of existing and of the establishment of an identity. (1990:151)

In summary, adolescents who remain overwhelmed with unbearable and unthinkable feelings because of early childhood traumas are left with a feeling of not existing as a real person. To survive, their energy goes into the creation of a false self. However, this could create an emotional breakdown and prevent them from functioning in the real world because of the fragility of their own real sense of self.

Without skilled care and treatment from workers who can recognise their emotional needs as continuing to feel lost and not provided for, their journey will take them towards mental health provision, rather than moving towards maturational individuation and into a world from which they can continue to develop emotionally.

> With extremes of abuse or neglect the long-term outcomes are far less hopeful than with mildly adverse circumstances, and children do not have as much potential for change. (Music 2011:236)

As mothers, carers or professionals responsible for helping the adolescents we know through their turbulent periods, we are surviving our own doldrums. By recognising and reflecting on the adolescent within us and how we found a way to endure our own difficult and painful parts during that period of our lives, we can develop our own insight and understanding as to how we can help, support and provide for the adolescent process of others.

Whether the adolescent is in an emotional state of integration or unintegration, it is possible for us to help them through their struggles and to manage their external world with success and satisfactory gain. To achieve this task, it is important that workers and carers recognise the starting point in their work and care for adolescents. Identifying adolescents who require continuing support through their maturation process and those who still require a form of primary provision, helping the fragmented child within them to feel emotionally contained and recognised, is critical.

CONCLUSION

Christine Bradley

The purpose of this book has been to provide some insight and understanding for carers and workers as they reach out to children and young people, who because of their own early traumatic experiences are overwhelmed by unbearable feelings of panic, rage and unthinkable anxiety that have remained embedded in their inner world. While preparing to write this book, I reflected on my own professional experiences, wondering how I could use my own learning from working with emotionally fragmented children and young people and providing them with therapeutic care and treatment programmes planned to meet their unmet needs. During the early years of my work, I was advised and taught by mentors who helped me to understand at a deeper level, and with a greater clarity, how I should interact and respond to traumatised children appropriately when meeting their needs. I have considered how I could help others to develop their practice, skills and knowledge base to provide therapeutic care and treatment for the children and young people for whom they are responsible. This foundation is at the heart of this book. It has been written to provide further insight and understanding about the complex interaction needed between the worker and child. It is hoped this will help workers to develop the skills needed when they experience being attacked and assaulted by the unbearable pain of the child's panic, rage and unthinkable anxiety, and as they attempt to reach out to them.

Providing the appropriate care and treatment patterns for workers, and developing methods of therapeutic practice, is crucial if they are to reach an understanding about their role in helping these children and young people whose life experiences have been so traumatic that their emotions remain stuck in their inner world. Such trauma can rupture and interrupt their transitions from early childhood and infancy through to later maturational development in their life. This can make it very difficult for them to function in the external world of reality. As a result, the young person cannot defend their developing sense of self because they have to survive their own unbearable feelings. The repercussions are far reaching, and can result in them becoming destructive, self-destructive or malevolent in their behaviour towards others and themselves. A deeper understanding of the role of assessment and treatment programmes will help carers and workers to manage young people's behaviour.

This book aims to give workers the opportunity to enter into a more creative phase of work and practice with abused and traumatised children. We are living in a culture where the increasing demand for outcomes and evidence-based practice can prevent real and meaningful communication from occurring, and prevent the development of creative solutions for engaging with difficult-to-reach children and young people who have never been able to express themselves other than through destructive or self-destructive behaviour.

The culture we live in is complex – it is multi-racial and multi-cultural, with reconstituted families, combined with many single parents who struggle with the burden of managing personally, practically and financially. There are parents who have problems with drug and alcohol abuse, and there is a high amount of domestic violence. There are child migrants who have witnessed death and war and find themselves either with extended family members or alone. How can professionals begin to think in the midst of all this? It is little wonder that we have higher numbers of children requiring specialist care and that the level of emotional damage in them is higher, deeper and more complex than it was for children 20 years ago. What this book has highlighted is that it is possible to achieve change in the lives of these children and young people, helping them to feel better about themselves, but only when the compassion, determination and commitment to endure the highs and lows of the work are acknowledged.

This change was described in the preface detailing the move at the Cotswold Community from an approved school to a therapeutic community. It highlighted that it was possible to achieve a new order for the children, but not without the workers enduring a high level of bearable and unbearable factors during the process of change. However, it also documented the outcome of defining a primary task based on the emotional needs of the children which could be implemented and used in the practice of the worker. The result was a better outcome for the children, after they were able to establish relationships with the workers that felt meaningful and real. This book has provided a historical account that examines the growth of two therapeutic communities and the struggles and determination that therapeutic change in organisations requires, if the insight and understanding gained from workers can be used in their working environment.

The book has also explored the concepts of integration and unintegration that have emerged from the work of Dockar-Drysdale and Winnicott, bringing together a deeper understanding about these underlying concepts and their impact on the sense of self of the child or young person. The use of the assessment of need and therapeutic treatment programmes offers a way forward for carers, workers and other professionals who are working with emotionally fragmented children and young people. Reflective thinking and open communication in the work between workers and children or young people, and staff teams in groups, is essential when identifying creative ways forward. Being emotionally contained and supported through supervision and consultation is an important part of the process for workers.

So having read the book, where does this leave the reader? How do they go ahead and place the theoretical concepts into working practice? It is possible to create ways of understanding and responding to the inner world of unintegrated children and young people and to plan patterns of care and treatment which can reach out to the more unbearable parts of their personality. To begin, the following question needs to be asked:

> What is the quality of culture in the home and therapeutic environment we are working in?

Before engaging with the therapeutic task, workers, children and young people need to experience an established culture, one which is a living and working environment, shared by all the members of the community. The following points are important for this:

1. The primary task needs to be defined, together with an understanding of the secondary needs, as the child or young person begins to embark on their maturational development.

2. Workers should receive ongoing training relating to the concept of integrated and unintegrated states in children and young people, with a resource of training material to be used.

3. Assessment of need and therapeutic treatment programmes should be used consistently with all children and young people resident in the home, measuring their emotional development.

4. Workers need to receive ongoing support, supervision and consultation to help them 'bear the unbearable' in their work with unintegrated children.

5. The organisation as a whole needs to be committed to the achievement of the therapeutic task, and meeting the emotional needs of integrated and unintegrated children and young people.

I have aimed to provide a model of working which makes life and living more bearable rather than consistently unbearable for workers, children and young people together.

Finally, I cannot complete this book without paying tribute to the work of my early mentors who inspired me greatly: Barbara Dockar-Drysdale, Richard Balbernie and, briefly, Dr Donald Winnicott. Both Richard Balbernie and Barbara Dockar-Drysdale held the belief, commitment and determination that if you believed a piece of work was worth struggling with to achieve, it would work. They each proved this to be the case with their work, Balbernie at the Cotswold Community, taking it through the fundamental changes it needed, and Dockar-Drysdale through her creation of the Mulberry Bush School in Oxfordshire. As the driving force of each of the therapeutic communities, they were highly creative and deeply focused on the task in hand. With their insight, reflexivity and understanding, they were deeply inspirational and often challenging. This was understood by those who worked with them, and almost to be expected when they held such compassion for and commitment to the task in hand.

Although as I have mentioned in the book the era of therapeutic communities during the 1970s, 1980s and 1990s has gone, the

Mulberry Bush School has managed to survive the passage of time and continues to develop and grow. Although adaptation to change is always required, and can be difficult and painful to achieve while adhering to changes in policy, the Mulberry Bush School has been able to hold on to the underlying analytical thinking and philosophical understanding of Dockar-Drysdale. It is interesting that, as I write, the Mulberry Bush School is about to celebrate its 70th anniversary. As Winnicott said to me in my early days, 'It is better not always to know; if we can afford to not know, the real knowing comes forward with meaning and sincerity.'

Afterword: The 'Someone' Involved in the Young Person's Care

Policy Aspects for Developing Facilitating and Holding Environments

Jonathan Stanley

This afterword continues the focus on the importance of the parenting relationship and considers the importance of policy in enabling relationships, taking a role as 'someone' involved in a young person's care.

Winnicott wrote, 'The centre of gravity of the being does not start off in the individual. It is in the total set up', observing, 'There is no such thing as a baby…if you show me a baby you certainly show me someone caring for the baby' (1978:99). Given that young people who are the focus of this book will also have the state as a 'corporate parent', with the state taking some responsibility for the welfare of the child through care orders or similar, it is important that the role of the state is considered in determining their potential in the development of the therapeutic relationship.

The 'holding' of an environment as described in this book is not solely at a personal level but necessarily is operating at policy and political levels; these intervene at the personal level. The needs of the young person are to be met personally, but the possibility of doing so can be enabled or restricted by what is in the policy. There is a wider psychological task and responsibility to be accepted by those acting at the level of the making of policy. There has to be a golden thread that runs from the personal (what is going to go on between the parent and child) and the policy (what is going on between the government, in the embodiment of a minister or department, and the development of children in general and for each child specifically).

Theirs is a social role, inextricably involved with the dynamics of the care system, not standing separate. Importantly there needs to be an acknowledgment that holding and leadership are not the same, but complementary. To achieve both, policy has to enable creativity of response rather than compliance by those it directs, working from growth rather than conformity to a prescribed standard.

Policy has to be conscious of its determining role of potential in caring environments. Being conscious can lead to affirmation or denial whereby affirmation enables the state by its actions to intervene to facilitate the therapeutic relationship actively beyond instrumental caring; and denial (taking a perspective that the authorities and state have no place in family life) is consciously restrictive by omission through a lack of intervention as a result of any such action being outside governmental remit – an assumption that the market will provide therapeutic resources. The English experience is that it does to a degree; but that the numbers are small and the intensive provision costs are factors that deter investment. Active governmental intervention is necessary.

Just as we have seen in this book that therapeutic space between a parent and a child has to be consciously created, so the state has to be conscious of its involvement in the therapeutic alliance between parent and child. It is not a factor that can be disregarded. Just as in the personal relationship the parent is acting to support moves from unintegration to integration by preoccupation creating ego-functioning and keeping the child 'in mind', so too the state has to ensure there is not the potential for children 'falling out of mind'. Any such latter situation could allow regressive dynamics or poor practice, i.e. acting outside evidence or sound experience, to operate.

Policy needs to be universal and individual. We can construct three categories of young people who become involved with the care system – namely: children with relatively simple or straightforward needs who require either short-term or relatively 'ordinary' substitute care; children or families with deep-rooted, complex or chronic needs with a long history of difficulty and disruption, including abuse or neglect, requiring more than simply a substitute family; and finally, children with extensive, complex and enduring needs compounded by very difficult behaviour who require more specialised and intensive resources such as a therapeutic residential children's home, an adolescent mental health setting, or a secure accommodation.

Seeking to provide a universal policy can focus most on the first grouping, so investing in early intervention and fostering. The next group is smaller and more challenging to accept as a reality, hence the need for professional experience and personal insight by policy makers. This group presents a challenge to universal services whose capabilities necessarily are not set up to meet these more intensive needs. That a child may need to move from the first group to the second or third group, perhaps rapidly, is the result of a failure to assess and place correctly. This can be a result of failure of policy to adequately include these groups in their thinking, resulting in a lack of holding of the facilitating environment, the necessary provision to meet their needs. These latter groups present a challenge to the imagination of policy and to the public purse to create responses that enable these young people to experience a more stable life within which they can grow and function into adulthood.

As this book shows, we have to be alive to there being a group of young people who can be seen to be in a 'pre-attachment' state. Not to incorporate this insight into policy is not to be meeting the needs as they are but as one would like them to be. It is important to appreciate the differing insights of Bowlby and Winnicott included in this book. Ordinary devoted parenting, required for some young people, is not the same as therapeutic parenting required by others. Conflating the two could lead in policy terms to there being one training or qualification with an assumption that one is the extension of the other, whereas this book shows the need for a distinct and specific professional development that addresses pre-attachment and unintegration.

Policy is required to recognise and act to ensure a range of substitute and supplemental placement options. A key requirement of central policy and practice is that assessment should be child focused to support appropriate provision for the child. For some young people, a foster family is not the 'right place at the right time'; some need specialist and intensive intervention, perhaps an early placement in a children's home. Planning requires that placement demand and supply are built on a need analysis – policy needs to ensure we have the provision needed where we need it. In these economic times, establishing new provision requires a solid business case. On the basis of sound assessment of needs, establishing demand and trend, providers and the state can create the holding environment necessary through a shared, open, mutual, transparent, collaborative, co-production relationship with parents. The ambition to be achieved for policy is for all children to 'develop a belief that the world can contain what is wanted and needed, with the result that the baby has hope and that there is a live relationship between inner reality and external reality' (Winnicott 1957:90).

Young people with the depth of needs described in this book are always with us. This makes the thinking and practice presented in this book eternally relevant. The book offers social workers, residential child care workers, foster carers, youth workers, teachers, psychologists, psychiatrists and therapists an insight into the emotional world of fragmented children and provides a framework of thinking that enables them to evaluate and provide for their development. It also offers an opportunity for professional practice to redefine needs and address gaps and spaces in children's services.

Glossary

Anti-social tendency, the

The anti-social tendency is connected to the concept of holding. Children and young people are thought to be looking for a sense of secure holding they find lacking in their family and furthermore in most sections of society at large. Winnicott considered anti-social behaviour as a cry for help, fuelled by a sense of loss of integrity, and without a sense of self the children felt comfortable with. It is often caused when the familial holding environment is inadequate or fragmented. The anti-social tendency has a failure to conform with social norms, with a lack of remorse from the children for their behaviour, with little or no sense of personal responsibility for their actions.

Boundaries

A boundary defines physical, symbolic or emotional territory. These boundaries must be managed effectively to maintain healthy functioning. Unintegrated children who have been exposed to physical and emotional abandonment in their early years find it difficult to maintain their boundaries and are overwhelmed by their emotions, losing a sense of their own and others' boundaries. Workers can help to manage the external boundaries without recourse to punishment, control, rewards or sanctions.

Counter-transference

The term denotes feelings which workers transfer from their past experiences, projecting these onto the problems of the child, thereby distorting their perception of the child's transferred feelings. It is important that workers can reflect on how the child or young person makes them feel after a difficult time. An understanding of their own emotions and the concept of counter-transference can help provide an insight into the child's emotions and develop the 'here and now' relationship between the worker and child or young person.

Fragile integration

A fragile integrated child is one who is beginning to come together as a person, having reached a stage in their development where they have a sense of self. Although at times of stress they can fall apart for a short while, they are able to recover with support and learn from painful experiences. They are ready to make attachment relationships with their workers, but still need considerable emotional support. Here the descriptive terms of frozen, archipelago and caretaker child have been superseded by emotional integration, which at times of stress, because of its fragility, can cause the child to revert to one of these earlier states.

Functioning

The functioning child can perform a task, meeting the expectations of others without breaking down and managing and resolving any challenges presented. These experiences help establish the foundation for maturational development. Functioning can break down when stress factors become overwhelming. Support from another can help maintain positive functioning.

Mentalising

Mentalising is the term given to the emotional understanding of and attunement to the mental states of one's self and others – to empathise and to see things from the perspective of others, an aspect that is critical in enabling social relationships.

Merging

Merging results when all sense of boundaries between self and others is non-existent or temporarily lost. This results in an over-identification between two or more children, leading to a single self through a 'primary' merger. Unintegrated children are vulnerable to merging and, when they do, results in a powerful and destructive force, which will resist any attempt to break up the merger. Their inability to take responsibility for their individual actions can lead to dangerous acting out regardless of their own safety or that of others.

Primary task

The main priority of work with children and young people is the primary task. This is identifying their emotional needs and the appropriate provision and support they require to meet those needs. For example, with a frozen child the primary task is to identify the primary needs they did not receive as a small child and for the worker to provide a structure which can meet and provide for them. Emotional growth can begin to develop after the task has been completed and the child feels genuinely provided for and emotionally contained. At this stage the primary task needs to be moved to the secondary task. The worker begins to strengthen the child or young person's emotional life as they begin to face reality.

Projective identification

What we cannot stand about ourselves we project onto others, identifying with what we consider to be parts of the other person. A child or young person could project their feelings of hopelessness and helplessness onto their carer, which could result in the carer not being able to contain the child or young person. When they become overwhelmed with their unbearable feelings which are part of the child or young person's unconscious fantasy, it can result in the child, young person or carer breaking down and ceasing to function.

Provision of primary experience

This describes the initial experience that takes place between a mother and an infant. It is intensely personal and reassures the infant that they are held in mind during their early development. An unintegrated child, however, having missed out on this experience, will experience a gap at the core of their existence, and this is normally bridged through the use of a transitional object.

Self-destruction and self-preservation

If a child has no sense of self-esteem they often are unable to take care of themselves. Their level of despair is so great that they react by turning on themselves after a period of acting out their anger and panic. Workers need to enable the child to feel emotionally contained and to nurture them through their difficult periods of hopelessness and helplessness.

Syndrome

The term syndrome describes a group of symptoms that collectively characterise a disease, disorder or condition.

Transference

Transference describes the process by which the child transfers onto their workers feelings and ideas which belong to previous figures in their life. They behave as though the worker were that person, with feelings being either positive or negative. It is important that the worker has some insight into who the child is trying to create, and not allow themselves to become that person. This insight will help the worker to understand the roots of the child's behaviour and to respond appropriately.

References

Abram, J. (1996) *The Language of Winnicott*. London: Karnac Books.

Adler, G. (1972) 'Helplessness in the helpers.' *British Journal of Medical Psychology*, 45, 315.

Allen, J.G. and Fonagy, P. (2006) *Handbook of Mentalization-Based Treatment*. Chichester: John Wiley.

Allen, J.G., Fonagy, P. and Bateman, A.W. (2008) *Mentalising in Clinical Practice*. Arlington, USA: American Psychiatric Publishing.

Anglin, J.P. (2003) 'A framework for understanding and practice in residential group care.' *Child and Youth Care*, 21 (10), 4–7.

Anglin, J.P. and Miller, R. (n.d.) *Providing Quality Residential Care for Young People, and Responding to the Sexual Exploitation of Our Vulnerable Youth*. Available at: www.iss-bg.org/pic/Providing_Quality_Residential_Care_for_Young_People.pdf, accessed on 4 September 2017.

Axline, V.M. (1990) *Dibs in Search of Self*. London: Penguin.

Ayre, D., Capron, L., Egan, H., French, A. and Gregg, L. (2016) *The Cost of Being Care Free: The Impact of Poor Financial Education and Removal of Support on Care Leavers*. London: The Children's Society.

Bach, R. (1972) *Jonathan Livingston Seagull*. London: HarperElement.

Balbernie, R. (1966) *Residential Work with Children*. London: Pergamon Press.

Balbernie, R. (1971) 'The impossible task.' Unpublished paper delivered to the Reading branch of the British Association of Social Workers, 22 October.

Bateman, A. and Fonagy, P. (2012) *Handbook of Mentalising in Mental Health*. Arlington, USA: American Psychiatric Publishing.

Bettelheim, B. (1950) *Love Is Not Enough: The Treatment of Emotionally Disturbed Children*. Glencoe, USA: Free Press.

Bettelheim, B. and Sylvester, H. (1948) 'A therapeutic milieu.' *American Journal of Psychiatry*, 18, 191–206.

Bowlby, J. (1988) *A Secure Base: Parent–Child Attachment and Healthy Human Development*. London: Routledge.

Bradley, C. (1997) 'Antisocial Tendency.' In E.V. Welldon (ed.) *A Practical Guide to Forensic Psychotherapy*. London: Jessica Kingsley Publishers.

Bradley, C. (2010) *Bearing the Unbearable*. Maidstone: Plant Pot.

Cameron, C., Connelly, G. and Jackson, S. (2015) *Educating Children and Young People in Care: Learning Placements and Caring Schools*. London: Jessica Kingsley Publishers.

Cooper, A. and Redfern, S. (2016) *Reflective Parenting: A Guide to Understanding What's Going On in Your Child's Mind*. Oxford: Routledge.

Dethiville, L. (2008) *Donald D. Winnicott: A New Approach*. London: Karnac Books.

Dockar-Drysdale, B. (1958) 'The Residential Treatment of Frozen Children.' In *Therapy and Consultation in Child Care*. London: Free Association.

Dockar-Drysdale, B. (1973) 'Staff Consultation in an Evolving Care System.' In *Residential Establishments: The Evolving of Caring Systems*. Conference Report, University of Dundee.

Dockar-Drysdale, B. (1988) 'The Difference between Child Care and Therapeutic Management.' In B. Dockar-Drysdale, *The Provision of Primary Experience*. London: Free Association, 1990.

Dockar-Drysdale, B. (1990) *The Provision of Primary Experience*. London: Free Association.

Dockar-Drysdale, B. (1958) 'Residential Treatment of "Frozen" Children.' In B. Dockar-Drysdale *Therapy and Consultation in Child Care*, London: Free Association Books, 1993.

Emond, R., Steckley, L. and Roesch-Marsh, A. (2016) *A Guide to Therapeutic Child Care*. London: Jessica Kingsley Publishers.

Felitti, V.J. and Anda, R.F. (2009) 'The Relationship of Adverse Childhood Experiences to Adult Health, Well-Being, Social Function, and Healthcare.' In R. Lanius and E. Vermetten (eds) *The Hidden Epidemic: The Impact of Early Life Trauma on Health and Disease*. Cambridge: Cambridge University Press.

Fonagy, P. (2000) 'Attachment and borderline personality disorder.' *Journal of the American Psychoanalytic Association*, 48 (4), 1129–1146; discussion 1175–1187.

Fonagy, P. and Luyten, P. (2009) 'A developmental, mentalization-based approach to the understanding and treatment of borderline personality disorder.' *Development and Psychopathology*, 21 (4), 1355–1381.

Fonagy, P. and Target, M. (1997) 'Attachment and reflective function: their role in self-organization.' *Development and Psychopathology*, 9 (4), 679–700.

Fonagy, P. (2001) *Attachment Theory and Psychoanalysis*. London: Karnac Books.

Fonagy, P., Gergely, G., Jurist, E. and Target, M. (2005) *Affect Regulation, Mentalization, and the Development of the Self*. New York, USA: Other Press.

Fonagy, P., Leigh, T., Steele, M., Steele, H. *et al.* (1996) 'The relation of attachment status, psychiatric classification, and response to psychotherapy.' *Journal of Consulting and Clinical Psychology*, 64, 22–31.

Fonagy, P., Steele, M., Steele, H., Higgit, A. and Target, M. (1994) 'The Emanuel Memorial Lecture 1992: the theory and practice of resilience.' *Journal of Child Psychology and Psychiatry*, 35 (2), 231–257.

Fonagy, P., Target, M., Gergely, G., Allen, J. and Bateman, A. (2003) 'The developmental roots of borderline personality disorder: a theory and some evidence.' *Psychoanalytic Inquiry*, 23, 412–458.

George, C. and Solomon, J. (2008) 'The Caregiving System: A Behavioral Systems Approach to Parenting.' In J. Cassidy and P.R. Shaver (eds) *Handbook of Attachment: Theory, Research, and Clinical Applications* (2nd edition). New York, USA: Guilford Press.

Gergely, G. and Watson, J. (1996) 'The social biofeedback theory of parental affect-mirroring: the development of emotional self-awareness and self-control in infancy.' *The International Journal of Psychoanalysis*, 77 (6), 1181–1212.

Giono, J. (1985) *The Man Who Planted Trees*. London: Peter Owen Publishers.

Griffin, J.E. and Ojeda, S.R. (eds) (1996) *Textbook of Endocrine Physiology*. New York, USA: Oxford University Press.

Hardwick, A. and Woodhead, J. (eds) (1992) *Loving, Hating and Surviving: Handbook for All Who Work with Troubled Children and Young People*. Aldershot: Ashgate.

Hauptmann, B. and Reeves, C. (2005) *Donald Winnicott and John Bowlby: Personal and Professional Perspectives*, ed. J. Issroff. London: Karnac Books.

Hinshelwood, R.D. (1987) *Staff as the Transference Object: What Happens in Groups*. London: Free Association.

Hirschorn, L. (1997) *Reworking Authority*. Cambridge, USA: The MIT Press.

Howe, D. (2011a) *Attachment Across the Lifecourse: A Brief Introduction*. Basingstoke: Palgrave Macmillan.

Howe, D. (2011b) *The Child's World*. London: Jessica Kingsley Publishers.

Huffington, C. (2004) 'What Women Leaders Can Tell Us.' In C. Huffington, D. Armstrong, W. Halton, L. Hoyle and J. Pooley (eds) *Working Below the Surface: The Emotional Life of Contemporary Organizations*. London: Karnac Books.

Leadsom, A., Field, F., Burstow, P. and Lucas, C. (2013) *The 1001 Critical Days: The Importance of Conception to the Age of Two Period*. Available at: www.wavetrust.org, accessed on 20 February 2017.

Lyons-Ruth, K., Dutra, L., Schuder, M.R. and Bianchi, I. (2006) 'From infant attachment disorganization to adult dissociation: relational adaptations or traumatic experiences?' *Psychiatric Clinics of North America*, 29, 63–86.

McCrory, E.J. and Viding, E. (2015) 'The theory of latent vulnerability: Reconceptualizing the link between childhood maltreatment and psychiatric disorder.' *Development and Psychopathology*, 27 (2), 493–505.

McCrory, E.J., De Brito, S., Kelly, P., Bird, G. *et al.* (2013) 'Amygdala activation in maltreated children during pre-attentive emotional processing.' *British Journal of Psychiatry*, 202 (4), 269–276.

McMahon, L. (1992) *A Handbook of Play Therapy*. London: Routledge.

Miller, E.J. (1986) 'Dedication and Charisma: An Appreciation of Richard William Balbernie, 3 July 1986.' Available at: www.johnwhitwell.co.uk/index.php/richard-balbernie, accessed on 14 March 2017.

Miller, E.J. (1989) 'Towards an Organisational Model for the Residential Treatment of Adolescents.' In C. Kaneklin and A. Orsenigo (eds) *Comunita Rezidentiala per Adolescenti Difficili*. Roma: Nuova Italia Scientific.

Music, G. (2011) *Nurturing Nature*. Brighton: Psychology Press.

Nagy, E., Pilling, K., Orvos, H. and Molnar, P. (2013) 'Imitation of tongue protrusion in human neonates: specificity of the response in a large sample.' *Developmental Psychology*, 49 (9), 1628–1638.

Oehlberg, B. (2008) 'Why schools need to be trauma informed.' *Trauma and Loss: Research and Interventions*, 8 (2), 1–4.

Perry, B.D. (1996) *Maltreated Children: Experience, Brain Development and the Next Generation*. New York and London: W.W. Norton.

Perry, B.D. (2006) 'Applying Principles of Neurodevelopment to Clinical Work with Maltreated and Traumatized Children: The Neurosequential Model of Therapeutics.' In N. Boyd (ed.) *Traumatized Youth in Child Welfare*. New York: Guilford Press.

Perry, B.D. and Hambrick, E. (2008) 'The neurosequential model of therapeutics.' *Reclaiming Children and Youth*, 17 (3), 38–43.

Pollak, S.D., Cicchetti, D., Hornung, K. and Reed, A. (2000) 'Recognizing emotion in faces: developmental effects of child abuse and neglect.' *Developmental Psychology*, 36, 679–688.

Raine-D'Antonio, T. (2004) *The Velveteen Principle*. Deerfield Beach, USA: Health Communication Inc.

Redl, F. and Wineman, D. (1951) *Children Who Hate*. Glencoe, USA: The Free Press.

Reeves, C. (2001) 'Minding the child: the legacy of Mrs. Dockar-Drysdale.' *Emotional and Behavioural Difficulties*, 6 (4), 213–235.

Rice, A.K. (1968) *Working Note No. 1*. Centre for Applied Social Research. London: Tavistock Institute.

Rose, M. (1990) *Healing Hurt Minds – The Peper Harow Experience*. London and New York, USA: Routledge/Tavistock.

Rustin, M. and Rustin, M. (1966) *Narratives of Love and Loss*. London: Karnac Books.

Rutter, M. (2006) *Genes and Behavior: Nature–Nurture Interplay Explained*. Oxford: Blackwell Publishers.

Salzberger-Wittenberg, I. (1999) *Psycho-Analytic Insight and Relationships*. Suffolk: Routledge and Kegan Paul.

Schechter, D.S., Myers, M., Brunelli, S., Coates, S. *et al.* (2006) 'Traumatized mothers can change their minds about their toddlers: understanding how a novel use of videofeedback supports positive change of maternal attributions.' *Infant Mental Health Journal*, 27, 429–447.

Schofield, G. and Beek, M. (2014) *Promoting Attachment and Resilience. A Guide for Foster Carers and Adopters on Using the Secure Base Model*. London: BAAF.

Schore, A.N. (1994) *Affect Regulation and the Origin of the Self: The Neurobiology of Emotional Development*. Mahwah, USA: Erlbaum.

Senecky, Y., Agassi, H., Inbar, D., Horesh, N. et al. (2009) 'Post-adoption depression among adoptive mothers.' *Journal of Affective Disorders*, 115, 62–68.

Slade, A. (2005) 'Parental reflective functioning: an introduction.' *Attachment and Human Development*, 7 (3), 269–281.

Steele, H. and Steele, M. (2005) 'Understanding and Resolving Emotional Conflict: The View from 12 Years of Attachment Research Across Generations and Across Childhood.' In K.E. Grossmann, K. Grossmann and E. Waters (eds) *Attachment from Infancy to Adulthood: The Major Longitudinal Studies*. New York, USA: Guilford Press.

Stein, P. and Kendall, J. (2004) *Psychological Trauma and the Developing Brain: Neurologically Based Interventions for Troubled Children*. New York, USA: Routledge.

Tagore, R. (1913) 'On the Seashore.' In *The Crescent Moon*. London and New York, USA: Macmillan and Company.

Teicher, M., Andersen, S., Polcari, A., Anderson, C., Navalta, C. and Kim, D. (2003) 'The neurobiological consequences of early stress and childhood maltreatment.' *Neuroscience and Biobehavioural Reviews*, 27 (1–2), 33–44.

Tomlinson, P. (2004) *Therapeutic Approaches in Work with Traumatised Children and Young People*. London: Jessica Kingsley Publishers.

Trevarthen, C., Delafield-Butt, J. and Schögler, B. (2011) 'Psychobiology of Musical Gesture: Innate Rhythm, Harmony and Melody in Movements of Narration.' In A. Gritten and E. King (eds) *Music and Gesture II*. Aldershot: Ashgate.

Tronick, E. (2007) *The Neurobehavioral and Social-Emotional Development of Infants and Children*. New York, USA: W.W. Norton.

Tronick, E., Als, H., Adamson, L., Wise, S. and Brazelton, T.B. (1978) 'Infants' response to entrapment between contradictory messages in face-to-face interaction.' *Journal of the American Academy of Child and Adolescent Psychiatry*, 17, 1–13.

Trowell, J. (2011) *Childhood Depression*. London: Karnac Books.

van der Kolk, B. (2014) *The Body Keeps the Score: Brain, Mind, and Body in the Healing of Trauma*. London: Penguin.

Waddell, M. (2002) *Inside Lives: Psychoanalysis and the Growth of the Personality*. London: Karnac Books.

Watt, D. (2000) 'The dialogue between psychoanalysis and neuroscience: alienation and reparation.' *Neuro-Psychoanalysis*, 2, 183–192.

Whitwell, J. (1998) 'Management issues in milieu therapy: boundaries and parameters.' *Therapeutic Communities Journal*, 19 (2), 89–105.

Williams, G. (2002) *The Internal Landscape and Foreign Bodies*. London: Karnac Books.

Wills, D. (1971a) *Pioneer Work with Maladjusted Children*. London: Stales Press.

Wills, D. (1971b) *Spare the Child*. London: Penguin.

Winnicott, D.W. (1957) *Mother and Child: A Primer of First Relationships*. New York, USA: Basic Books.

Winnicott, D.W. (1958) 'Primary Maternal Pre-Occupation.' In *Through Paediatrics to Psychoanalysis*. London: Tavistock.

Winnicott, D.W. (1960) 'The theory of the parent–infant relationship.' *International Journal of Psycho-Analysis*, 41, 585–595.

Winnicott, D.W. (1965) *The Maturational Processes and the Facilitating Environment*. London: Hogarth Press and the Institute of Psychoanalysis.

Winnicott, D.W. (1968) *Playing and Reality*. London: Penguin.

Winnicott, D.W. (1970) David Wills lecture to AWMC, 23 October.

Winnicott, D.W. (1971) 'Transitional Objects and Transitional Phenomena.' In *Playing and Reality*. London: Tavistock.

Winnicott, D.W. (1973) *The Child, the Family, and the Outside World*. London: Penguin.

Winnicott, D.W. (1978) *Through Paediatrics to Psycho-Analysis*. London: Hogarth Press.

Winnicott, D.W. (1990) *The Maturational Processes and the Facilitating Environment*. London: Karnac Books.

Winnicott, D.W. (1997) *Deprivation and Delinquency*. London: Routledge.

List of Contributors

Author

Christine Bradley has worked in the field of psychotherapy both nationally and internationally in practice over the past 40 years. She was a principal officer for residential services for a local authority in London, and is a trainer and consultant to numerous local authorities and children's organisations. Her expertise lies in the fields of play and communication and working with practitioners to develop the skills and understanding needed to work with emotionally fragmented children and young people. She is a fellow of the Social Policy Group at Dartington Research Unit and has contributed many book chapters in addition to publishing *Bearing the Unbearable: Insight into the World of Emotionally Fragmented Children and Young People.*

Editor

Francia Kinchington is a principal lecturer and teaching fellow at the University of Greenwich in the Faculty of Education and Health. She is an education consultant with international expertise in leading and managing change and an experienced doctoral supervisor and examiner in the fields of education, psychology and health. She has an MA in Educational Psychology and is a graduate member of the British Psychological Society.

Contributors

Alistair Cooper is a clinical psychologist with over 12 years of experience of working with children and adolescents in care. He is the co-author of *Reflective Parenting: A Guide to Understanding What's Going*

On in Your Child's Mind, and delivers two training courses, which aim to help professionals increase the mentalising capacity of parents they are working with.

John Diamond is Chief Executive Officer of the Mulberry Bush Organisation, active member of the All Party Parliamentary Group for looked after children and care leavers and a trustee of the National Association of Special Schools. He is on the editorial board of the *International Journal of Therapeutic Communities*, and a member of the Therapeutic Communities Accreditation Panel at the Royal College of Psychiatrists.

Jonathan Stanley has been the principal partner since 2000 for the National Centre for Excellence in Residential Child Care (NCERCC), a main point of reference and dialogue for the residential sector of England, and is currently the Chief Executive Officer for the Independent Children's Homes Association in England. Prior to joining NCERCC, Jonathan worked in local authority, voluntary and independent sectors managing residential and associated integrated provision (education, care, health, therapy) for national psychosocial and psychotherapeutic resources addressing the learning, emotional and social needs of young people. In an expert advisory capacity, he works with national government and is a core member of the working group addressing the reform of residential child care and the required legislation. He regularly meets local government and the social care regulators, provides training and consultancy, and is sought after for contributions to various publications.

Judith Trowell is an honorary consultant child psychiatrist and former chair of the Child and Family Department at Tavistock Clinic, and Professor of Child Mental Health at the University of Worcester. She is a psychoanalyst, trustee of Coram and Coram Voice, and past chair and co-founder of YoungMinds. Her research includes psychotherapy outcome studies, adult mental health and child protection, and comparative outcome studies. Her training interests are court work and psychodynamic psychotherapy. She is a fellow of the Social Policy Group at Dartington Research Unit.

John Whitwell worked in the therapeutic social care sector from 1969 to 2014. He worked at the Cotswold Community, a pioneering therapeutic community for severely emotionally disturbed boys, from 1972 to 1999 and took over from Richard Balbernie as Principal in 1985. He qualified as a group-analytic psychotherapist in 1984 and in 1999 became Managing Director of the Integrated Services Programme, which provided therapeutic foster care for children and young people with complex needs. His publications focus on aspects of psychotherapeutic child care. Since retiring he has been involved as a trustee of three charities: The Mulberry Bush Organisation; Gloucestershire Counselling Service; and the Planned Environment Therapy Trust. He is a fellow of the Social Policy Group at Dartington Research Unit.

Index